**this book is from
the kitchen library of**

_____

ALSO BY ART GINSBURG, MR. FOOD®

The Mr. Food® Cookbook (1990)
Mr. Food® Cooks Like Mama (1992)
Mr. Food® Cooks Pasta (1993)
Mr. Food® Makes Dessert (1993)

MR. FOOD®
cooks
chicken

Art Ginsburg
MR. FOOD®

WILLIAM MORROW AND COMPANY, INC.
new york

Library of Congress Cataloging-in-Publication Data

Ginsburg, Art.
Mr. Food® cooks chicken / Art Ginsburg.
p.   cm.
Includes index.
ISBN 0-688-11600-0
1. Cookery (Chicken).   2. Cookery (Turkey).   I. Title.
TX750.5.C45G56 1993
641.6'65—dc20   93-8502
CIP

Printed in the United States of America

First Edition

1 2 3 4 5 6 7 8 9 10

BOOK DESIGN BY CHARLOTTE STAUB

4

Dedicated to
All those in food and on stage
Who've worked as hard as I have—
And have yet to realize their dreams,
as I have

acknowledgments

Anybody who thinks a cookbook is simply a collection of recipes thrown together should think again!

It's work, by a lot of people. Well, for instance . . .

My wife, Ethel, who not only helps with the recipe testing, but keeps me in line, too.

My son, Steve, who heads up everything for my books and handles everything that I could possibly think of—and everything else, too! He's the real boss.

My daughter-in-law, Carol, and daughter Caryl, who organize and make sense of the recipes and all of my words. Each time my scattered thoughts come together to become an entertaining, easy-to-follow book . . . it's because of Carol and Caryl.

Linda Rose, Steve Gershman, Alan Roer, Madeline Burgan, and Lori-ann Bishop, my recipe testers, who test and test until we're all certain that the recipes will work every time. Boy, do they have patience!

And Mary Ann Oliver! She types, copies, sorts, and does hundreds of things for us all, so that everything comes out right.

Roy Fantel and Tammy Ginsburg, who check up on all of us with their fine-tooth combs.

Chuck Ginsburg, Flo Toppal, Dan Wolk, and Bill Treacy, who make sure that we all have what we need at our fingertips, right when we need it.

I must also thank my agent, Bill Adler, without whose creativity, foresight, and guidance I wouldn't have written my books; and my editor, Maria Guarnaschelli, who, with a smile on her face and in her voice, encourages and supports me as she leads me to book-writing happiness; and Al Marchioni, Phyllis Heller, Skip Dye, and Larry Norton, the gang at William Morrow, who push harder for me than I do for myself—they're not only a publishing group, they're dedicated friends.

And there are more! But these people never get their names on the books like I do; they never get the credit they deserve. . . . Well, gosh! They just did, and am I glad—'cause to all these guys I owe a really big THANKS!

Thanks, also, to the companies, friends, and viewers who've graciously shared their recipes with me, including:

The National Broiler Council

Bertolli USA, Inc.

Filippo Berio Olive Oil

The Turkey Store

Pace Picante Sauce

Thomas J. Lipton Co.

Hidden Valley Ranch

Campbell Soup Co.

Kraft/General Foods, Inc.

Louis Rich

U.S.A. Rice Council

The North Carolina Department of Agriculture

The National Turkey Federation

Borden Inc.-Gioia

Australian Toaster® Biscuit

Pepperidge Farm, Inc.

Bisquick®, a registered trademark of General Mills, Inc.

Delmarva Poultry Industry, Inc.

Hellmann's & Best Foods Mayonnaise

Chef Normand Leclair of the Red Rooster Tavern

Alan Roer

Iris Spindel

Aileen Herbstman

Jack Urdang

Joni Leterman

contents

Acknowledgments 7

Introduction 11

charts and information 15

Chicken Buying Guide 17

Tips for Buying and Preparing Poultry 18

How Much Chicken to Buy 19

Boning and Cutting Diagrams 20

Timetable for Roasting Chicken 23

Roasting a Whole Turkey 24

Equivalents and Substitutions 27

Packaged Foods Note 28

beginnings 29

marinades, sauces, and other light 'n' easies 41

main courses 57

"one-pans" 103

taste adventures 119

family favorites 135

Index 149

introduction

"A chicken in every pot," "Sunday Chicken," "Holiday Chicken." Chicken has been at all our special events, so it's only natural that we love it so much.

Chicken is so popular that it has surpassed beef as the most consumed "meat." We can enjoy the whole chicken or just our favorite parts—and the part that nearly everyone wants is the chicken breast. It's the white meat we all used to fight for. The chicken processors report that over 50 percent of our chicken demand is for chicken breasts in some shape or form.

Because of the demand for breast meat, all the other parts have to be promoted at a lower price in order to stimulate their sale. So, the really super buys are for the legs, thighs, drumsticks, wings, necks, and, of course, whole chickens, too.

I still maintain that the easiest item to make is a whole roasted chicken. Wash it, sprinkle on a little salt and pepper, throw it into a 350°F. oven, and the oven does the rest. Isn't that easy? Sure, you can use other spices if you want, but salt and pepper, or even pepper alone, will do just fine.

Now, a lot that applies to chicken goes for turkey, too. We look forward to our cozy family gatherings so that we can have our old favorite. But turkey isn't just for holidays anymore.

Turkey is enjoying the same popularity today as chicken. It's relatively low in fat, fast-cooking, economical, versatile, and comes in lots of different forms and cuts. Whether we make it the traditional way, or use it ground for lighter burgers, meat loaf, or chili, there's lots we can do with it. Check out my note about flavoring ground turkey. . . . And check out all the creative ways with turkey that are included here. I know you'll be pleasantly surprised!

In days gone by, the farmers would sell their chickens to the local butchers only when they were no longer good for egg producing. The meat was far from tender and desirable. Fortunately for us, today our chicken supply is plentiful, and it's inspected and controlled under better conditions than ever.

Even so, there's always room for improvement. But we have to do our part. Salmonella and other bacteria can touch almost any of our foods. We need to be practical and take care in choosing and preparing our food, to minimize any risks. Please make careful note of my chart on buying and preparing poultry. There's a lot we can do to make our poultry healthy.

In my opinion, probably the most advanced health option we could demand now is the irradiation of our poultry. The only bad part of irradiation is its name. It conjures up unnecessary fear. A lot of people are afraid of it because they don't really understand it. It's simply using safe gamma rays to clean food of any bacteria that may be present. Would I eat irradiated poultry? Gladly. I think it's the healthiest poultry product yet.

I'm not maintaining that every piece of poultry should be irradiated, . . . because just as it should be available for those who want it, there should also be nonirradiated poultry for those who don't. But with all the ongoing advances in growing, feeding, transportation, refrigeration, and inspection methods, our final products keep getting better and better.

What can we do with it? What *can't* we do with it?! It's so versatile! Just from making chicken soup we get not only a pot full of rich chicken essence but cooked chicken for salads and sandwiches, quick casseroles . . . I could go on and on, and that's only the beginning of what we can do with *boiled* chicken!

We can bake, broil, roast, sauté, fry (and stir-fry), stuff, shred, top it . . . and then some!

And every way is good! Why, just imagine all the thousands of combinations! Any seasonings go with chicken, so we can get really creative. There are no rules. The recipes in this book have all kinds of special touches, from homestyle to fancy to ethnic. All of them are easy and no-nonsense, with few ingredients. I use no exotic, hard-to-get, expensive ingredients. Everything called for should already be in your cupboards, or is readily available from your local supermarket.

Most of these recipes are quick-cooking, with short preparation times. Chicken cooks fast. And when using only breast meat, it *really* cooks fast. . . . A few minutes is all it takes.

And if we're grilling our chicken, it sure makes a lot of sense to partially cook it in the oven and refrigerate it beforehand. That way it doesn't have to be on the grill so long, with the outside getting burned by the time the inside cooks through. If it's cooked ahead of time, you just have to add your barbecue or other sauce for the last ten minutes of grilling; you'll get the same finished barbecue taste with a lot better result. Try it . . . you'll see!

Nope, chicken and turkey aren't just for Sunday and holiday dinners anymore. So, jump in and enjoy. They're the meats of the future. Something nice to look forward to, hmm?!

Why not start now? With over one hundred popular, quick, and easy recipes, I know that this book won't get a chance to collect dust on your bookshelf. It's gonna be at your elbow, on your counter, ready to add novelty to your meals. Even if you use it just for ideas, that's fine. Any way you do it, you'll still be a kitchen hero! That should make you very happy. And when you're happy, I'm happy, 'cause you know what happy people say . . . Yup,

OOH it's so GOOD!!™

NOTE: Lots of people steer clear of ground turkey because they've found it to be kind of bland. Well, here's a helpful secret for getting the most from ground turkey: It must be seasoned more heavily than other ground meat. Use more salt, pepper, garlic and onion powders, or whatever seasonings you want—but use them generously so that you can have another way to enjoy turkey with new, full flavor. (Ground turkey cooks through faster than other ground meats, too.)

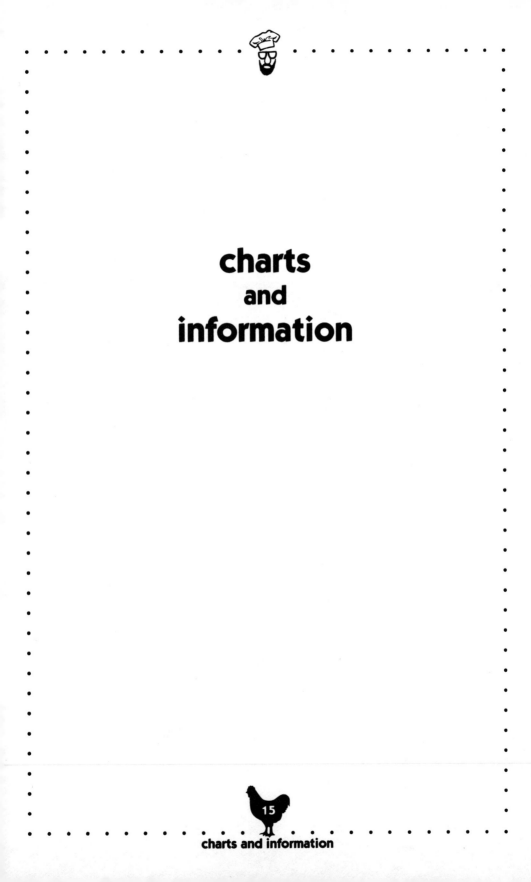

charts
and
information

chicken buying guide

Whole Broiler-Fryers: The most economical way to buy chicken. Cook whole or cut into serving-sized pieces. Usually packed with heart, liver, and gizzard (giblets) inside the carcass cavity. Usually weigh 2¾ to 4 pounds.

Young Roasters: Large, meaty birds usually packed with neck and giblets. Usually weigh 4½ to 6 pounds.

Cut-up Whole Chicken (Parts): A whole bird (with or without the neck and giblets) that has been cut into 4, 6, 8, or 9 pieces (drumsticks, thighs, breast halves, and wings). The back may be separate or part of the breast and thigh pieces.

Select Parts: May be purchased packaged together, making it easy for the consumer to buy only the family's favorite pieces or parts needed for a special recipe. Various combinations of packages include halves, quarters, drumsticks, thighs, breasts, wings, drummettes, and leg-thigh combinations.

Boneless Products: 100 percent edible, with bone removed before packaging; most popular with skin removed. Includes breasts (light meat) and thighs (dark meat), combination packs, nuggets, breast tenders, and cutlets.

Ground Chicken: Made primarily of thigh meat. Now widely available as a low-fat alternative to ground beef.

Partially Prepared Products: Boneless or bone-in parts that have been marinated or seasoned in some way, but not cooked.

Fully Cooked: Fresh whole broilers and/or parts that have been seasoned in a variety of ways, fully prepared, and sold ready to eat.

SOURCE: Courtesy of the National Broiler Council.

tips for buying
and preparing poultry

1. Shop at a reputable market, and be sure you're free to ask questions about its food-handling practices.

2. Buy your poultry (and meat) last so that it's not sitting in your basket while you do the rest of your shopping.

3. Choose product that is plump, clean, and free of bruises and discoloration. Skin color will vary depending upon the diet of the bird; it is not a measure of nutritional value, fat content, flavor, or tenderness. Avoid poultry with gray or pasty appearance and choose tightly wrapped packages free of tears. To ensure product freshness, note the "sell by" date on the package label. The date indicates the last day the product should appear in the meat case. One to two days beyond the date are allowed for safe refrigeration at home. For longer storage, the product should be frozen.

4. Take it directly home and put it in the refrigerator right away or freeze by individually wrapping large parts in freezer wrap or freezer bags. Wrap smaller pieces in serving-sized portions. Seal, label, and date each package. Poultry that has been commercially frozen can be kept in a home freezer for up to one year; noncommercially frozen poultry should be used within four to six months. Frozen cooked poultry should be used within two months.

5. Always thaw in the refrigerator, never at room temperature. Thawed poultry should be cooked promptly. (Whole chickens will take 12 to 16 hours to thaw; parts will thaw in 4 to 9 hours, depending on the size and number of parts in the package. For specific turkey thawing instructions, see the timetable for Roasting a Whole Turkey.) It is not recommended that either cooked or uncooked chicken be refrozen once it has been thawed.

6. Before cooking, rinse the poultry quickly under cold running water and pat dry with paper towels.

18

7. Use clean utensils, and wash any utensils that have been left out at room temperature or in the sun.

8. Do not use the same utensils or plates for raw and cooked items. Pay particular care to this point when using marinades and sauces—don't apply them to cooked items once they've come in contact with raw ones.

9. VERY IMPORTANT: Cook all poultry until it's completely cooked through. There's no such thing as cooking poultry to medium or medium-rare. Chicken is done when a meat thermometer inserted into the thickest part of the thigh registers 180°F., and boneless registers 160°F. It should be fork-tender and the juices should run clear, not pink.

10. Leftover cooked chicken may be safely kept in the refrigerator for 3 to 4 days. Cooked chicken nuggets or patties, 1 to 2 days.

11. When stuffing poultry, be sure to:
    - Refrigerate stuffing until ready to stuff and roast.
    - Adjust cooking time and temperature accordingly.
    - Remove leftover stuffing from bird immediately after dinner and refrigerate bird and stuffing separately.

how much chicken to buy

When buying chicken, keep in mind that an average serving* of

Whole Chicken	is	½ to ¾ pound
Breasts (with or without bone)	is	½ breast
Cutlets	is	1 cutlet
Legs (thighs and drumsticks attached)	is	1 leg
Thighs or Drumsticks	is	2 thighs or drumsticks
Wings	is	3 wings

*Serving size depends upon the other items being served with your meal, as well as the size of the chicken and, of course, the appetites!

SOURCE: Courtesy of Delmarva Poultry Industry, Inc.

boning and cutting diagrams

boning whole chicken breast

Some of the world's most elegant dishes are made with boned chicken breasts. For convenience, buy packaged breasts, already boned. For economy, bone them yourself.

1. Place skin-side down on cutting board with widest part nearest you. With point of knife, cut through white cartilage at neck end of keel bone.

2. Pick up breast and bend back, exposing keel bone.

3. Loosen meat from bone by running thumbs around both sides; pull out bone and cartilage.

4. Working with one side of breast, insert tip of knife under long rib bone inside thin membrane and cut or pull meat from rib cage. Turn breast and repeat on other side.

5. Working from ends of wishbone, scrape all flesh away and cut bone from meat. (If white tendons remain on either side of breast, loosen with knife and pull out.)

SOURCE: Courtesy of the National Broiler Council.

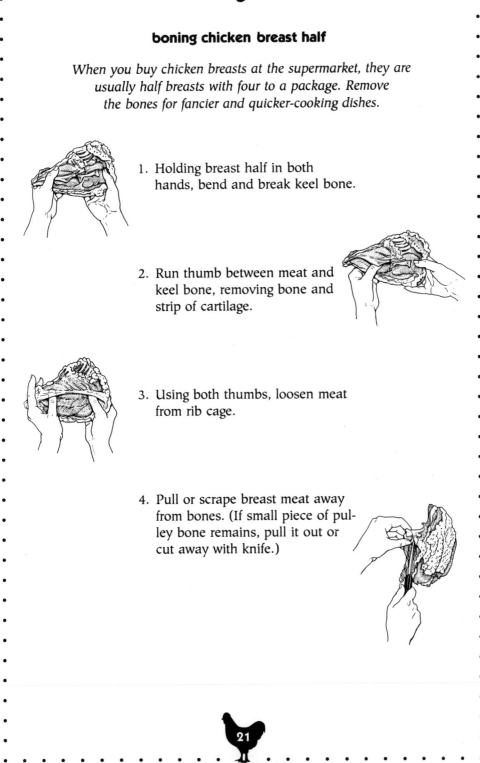

boning chicken breast half

*When you buy chicken breasts at the supermarket, they are
usually half breasts with four to a package. Remove
the bones for fancier and quicker-cooking dishes.*

1. Holding breast half in both
   hands, bend and break keel bone.

2. Run thumb between meat and
   keel bone, removing bone and
   strip of cartilage.

3. Using both thumbs, loosen meat
   from rib cage.

4. Pull or scrape breast meat away
   from bones. (If small piece of pul-
   ley bone remains, pull it out or
   cut away with knife.)

charts and information

cutting wing drummettes

Chicken drummettes, oven- or deep-fried, are favorite finger foods for party nibbling. And wings are one of the most economical chicken parts. Buy packaged drummettes or select wings and separate the meatier part, saving the wing tips for stock or soup.

1. With skin-side down, flatten wing on cutting board with wing tip on left and thicker (drummette) portion on right.

2. Cut through joint, leaving as much skin as possible on drummette.

timetable for roasting chicken
(at 350° f.)

PARTS	APPROXIMATE WEIGHT	FINAL MEAT THERMOMETER READING (IN DEGREES F.)	APPROXIMATE COOKING TIME* (IN MINUTES)
Whole			
unstuffed	3½ lbs.	185 to 190	1 hr. 15 min.
stuffed	3½ lbs.	185 to 190	1 hr. 40 min.
cut-up†	3½ lbs.	180	50 to 60
4 Thighs	4½ to 6½ oz. each	180	45 to 50
4 Thighs (boneless)	3½ to 5½ oz. each	160	30 to 35
4 Breast halves	8 to 10 oz. each	180	50 to 55
4 Breast halves (boneless)	5 to 7 oz. each	160	30 to 35
4 Drumsticks	3½ to 5½ oz. each	180	45 to 50
4 Leg-thigh combina-tions	8½ to 10½ oz. each	185 to 190	50 to 55
4 Quarters (2 breasts, 2 leg-thighs)	12 to 14 oz. each	185 to 190	60 to 65

*Cooking times are based on chicken taken directly from the refrigerator.

†Approximate weight of pieces of a cut-up 3½-lb. broiler-fryer chicken:
Thighs	5 to 6 oz. each
Drumsticks	3½ to 4 oz. each
Breasts with rib (halves)	9 to 10 oz. each
Wings	3 to 4 oz. each
Whole back	8 to 9 oz. each

SOURCE: Courtesy of the National Broiler Council.

roasting a whole turkey

As simple as 1-2-3!

Turkey is one of today's best meat buys, both nutritionally and economically. Whole turkeys are sold oven-ready: dressed, washed, inspected, and packaged. After turkeys leave the processing plant, no hands touch them until time for kitchen preparation.

It takes only 6 minutes to prepare a defrosted whole turkey for roasting (without stuffing).

If stuffing is desired, it's often best prepared separately, placed in a covered casserole, and cooked with the turkey during the last hour of roasting time.

Follow the label instructions for roasting, or use these simple directions to obtain a beautiful golden brown, ready-to-carve-and-eat turkey:

1. **Thawing:** (If turkey is not frozen, begin with step 2.) *Do not thaw poultry at room temperature.* Leave turkey in original packaging and use one of the following methods:

   No Hurry: Place wrapped turkey on a tray in the refrigerator for 3 to 4 days; allow 5 hours per pound of turkey to completely thaw.

   Fastest: Place wrapped turkey in the sink and cover with cold water. Allow about ½ hour per pound of turkey to completely thaw. Change the water frequently.

   Refrigerate or cook the turkey when it is thawed. Refreezing uncooked turkey is not recommended.
   Commercially frozen *stuffed* turkeys should *not* be thawed before roasting.

2. **Preparation for Roasting:** All equipment and materials used for storage, preparation, and serving of poultry must be clean. Wash hands thoroughly with hot soapy water before and after handling raw poultry. Use hard plastic or acrylic cutting boards to prepare poultry.

Remove the plastic wrapping from the thawed turkey. Remove the giblets and neck from the body and neck cavities. To remove the neck, it may be necessary to release the legs from the band of skin or wire hock lock. Rinse the turkey inside and out with cool water, pat dry with a paper towel, and return the legs to the hock lock or band of skin; or tie together loosely. Tuck the tips of the wings under the back of the turkey. The neck skin should be skewered with a poultry pin or round toothpick to the back of the turkey to provide a nice appearance for serving at the table. The turkey is now completely ready for roasting.

3. **Open Pan Roasting:** Place turkey breast-side up on a flat rack in a shallow roasting pan, about 2 inches deep. Insert the meat thermometer deep into the thickest part of the thigh next to the body, not touching the bone.

Brush the turkey skin with vegetable oil to prevent drying. If you'd like, sprinkle with salt, pepper, paprika, and any of your favorite poultry seasonings. (I especially like to add tarragon or thyme, and garlic and onion powders.) The same flavorings will work with turkey parts, too. Turkey is done when the meat thermometer registers 180 to 185°F. and the drumstick is soft and moves easily at joint.

Once the skin of the turkey is golden brown, shield the breast loosely with a rectangular-shaped piece of lightweight foil to prevent overbrowning.

For bone-in parts, juices should run clear when the meat is pierced in the deepest part with a long-tined fork. Cooked turkeys should be allowed to stand for 10 to 20 minutes before carving.

Allow at least 1 to 1½ pounds of uncooked turkey per person when purchasing a whole turkey. (This allows for leftovers!)

SOURCE: Courtesy of the National Turkey Federation.

charts and information

timetable for
roasting a whole turkey (at 325° f.)

APPROXIMATE WEIGHT (IN POUNDS)	APPROXIMATE ROASTING TIME* (IN HOURS)
6 to 8	2¼ to 3¼
8 to 12	3 to 4
12 to 16	3½ to 4½
16 to 20	4 to 5
20 to 24	4½ to 5½

*Approximate Roasting Time: Factors affecting roasting times are type of oven, oven temperature, and degree of thawing. Begin checking turkey for doneness about 1 hour before end of recommended roasting time.

SOURCE: Courtesy of the National Turkey Federation.

equivalents and substitutions
quick measures

EQUALS

Dash	less than ⅛ teaspoon
3 teaspoons	1 tablespoon
4 tablespoons	¼ cup
5 tablespoons plus 1 teaspoon	⅓ cup
8 tablespoons	½ cup
10 tablespoons plus 2 teaspoons	⅔ cup
12 tablespoons	¾ cup
16 tablespoons	1 cup
2 tablespoons	1 fluid ounce
1 cup	½ pint or 8 fluid ounces
2 cups	1 pint or 16 fluid ounces
4 cups	2 pints or 1 quart or 32 fluid ounces
4 quarts	1 gallon or 64 fluid ounces
Juice of 1 lemon	about 3 tablespoons
Juice of 1 orange	about ½ cup
Grated peel of 1 lemon	about 1½ teaspoons
Grated peel of 1 orange	about 1 tablespoon

substitutions

1 Pound* of	Equals Approximately
Rice	2 cups
Macaroni	4 cups
Meat	2 cups chopped
Potatoes	2 cups diced or 2 large whole
Cheese	4 cups grated

*One pound equals 16 ounces avoirdupois (our usual standard of weight measurement).

substitutions

EQUALS

1 Pound* of	Equals Approximately
1 tablespoon dehydrated minced onion	¼ cup finely minced fresh onion
1 teaspoon onion powder	⅓ of an onion
⅛ teaspoon garlic powder	1 garlic clove
1 tablespoon dehydrated parsley flakes	2 tablespoons fresh minced parsley

packaged foods note

As with many processed foods, package sizes may vary by brand. Generally, the sizes indicated in these recipes are average sizes. If you can't find the exact indicated package size, whatever package is closest in size will usually do the trick.

beginnings

GARLIC CHICKEN BITES   31

CHICKEN PUFFS   32

SESAME CHICKEN   33

PARTY PIZZA   35

CREAMY TOMATO CHICKEN SPREAD   36

TURKEY STUFFED MUSHROOMS   37

GREEK SPINACH SOUP   38

GARLIC SOUP   39

PARSNIP AND SPINACH
CREAM SOUP   40

garlic chicken bites

about 25 pieces

They'll think you fussed, but you'll know the truth.

2   chicken breasts (about 1 pound), boned, skinned, and cut into bite-sized strips
½   cup olive oil

4   garlic cloves, minced
¼   teaspoon black pepper
½   cup dry bread crumbs
¼   teaspoon cayenne pepper

Place the chicken strips in a large shallow dish. In a small bowl, mix together the olive oil, garlic, and black pepper and pour over the chicken strips. Cover and let the chicken marinate in the refrigerator for 30 minutes; drain off excess marinade and discard. Preheat the oven to 475°F. In another shallow dish, mix the bread crumbs with the cayenne pepper; dip both sides of the chicken strips in the mixture. Arrange the strips in a single layer on a non-stick cookie sheet(s). Bake for about 10 minutes, or until browned.

chicken puffs

8 servings

This is leftover chicken at its best, and whether you serve these as pass-around appetizers or make them bigger and serve 2 on a plate as dinner appetizers, your company will think you started from scratch just for them!

2 small packages (3 ounces each) cream cheese, softened

5 tablespoons butter or margarine, melted and divided

2 cups diced cooked chicken

¼ cup milk

½ teaspoon pepper

2 tablespoons minced onion

2 tablespoons diced pimientos

2 cans (8 ounces each) crescent rolls

Preheat the oven to 350°F. In a large bowl, mix together the cream cheese and 3 tablespoons melted butter. Add the chicken, milk, pepper, minced onion, and pimientos; mix well. Separate each package of crescent rolls into four rectangles. Spoon the chicken filling into the center of each rectangle, distributing it evenly. Bring the ends up together and pinch closed. Brush with reserved 2 tablespoons of melted butter. Place the puffs on a greased cookie sheet and bake for 12 to 15 minutes, or until golden brown.

NOTE: You can use all white meat chicken, all dark, or a combination. . . . Whatever you have and prefer. And how 'bout adding a sprinkle of your favorite spice?

sesame chicken

about 25 pieces

Sounds exotic, doesn't it? Well, they may think it's a mystery from the Far East, so don't tell them the recipe if you can help it. Keep it a secret. . . . It makes for more fun!

MARINADE

1 cup white wine

1 cup bottled duck sauce

½ cup soy sauce

¼ teaspoon garlic powder, reconstituted with 1 tablespoon water

4 chicken breasts, split, skinned, boned, and cut into finger-sized pieces

2½ cups cornstarch

2 tablespoons sesame seed

Vegetable oil for frying

2 tablespoons orange juice or water

In a large bowl, mix together the marinade ingredients. Add the chicken fingers and marinate in the refrigerator, covered, for a minimum of 15 minutes or up to 1 hour. Reserve the marinade. In a shallow dish, combine the cornstarch and sesame seed. Remove the chicken fingers from the marinade, shaking them dry, and roll them in the cornstarch mixture. Reserve the cornstarch mixture. Place the coated chicken fingers on a cookie sheet or sheet of waxed paper; set aside. In a large skillet, heat ¼ to ½ cup vegetable oil over medium heat; add a handful of chicken fingers and stir-fry quickly, about 4 to 5 minutes, or until golden.

Remove the chicken and drain on paper towels; repeat the process, adding more oil as needed, until all chicken fingers have been stir-fried. Keep warm. In a small bowl, mix together 1 tablespoon of the reserved cornstarch mixture with the orange juice; set aside. Place the reserved marinade in a medium-sized saucepan, and bring to a boil over a medium-high heat. Add the cornstarch mixture and continue cooking until the sauce has thickened, about 1

(continued)

33

beginnings

minute, stirring constantly. Place the chicken fingers on a serving platter and drizzle with the sauce.

NOTE: If you really want to make your dish look fancy, place the chicken fingers on a bed of peeled seedless orange slices. This is a great one to make ahead—just reheat the chicken fingers and rewarm the sauce. And if you want to make this as a main course, it'll make 4 to 6 servings.

party pizza
about 8 servings

*Having friends over? Make something that you can't get
at a pizza parlor. It's yours alone!*

1 pound Italian turkey sausage or sweet or hot Italian sausage, casing removed, crumbled

1 can (6 ounces) tomato paste

1 can (8 ounces) tomato sauce

1 can or jar (about 4 ounces) mushroom slices and pieces, drained

1 garlic clove, minced

½ teaspoon dried oregano

⅛ teaspoon salt

⅛ teaspoon pepper

1 loaf party rye or French bread, cut in half lengthwise

1 cup (4 ounces) shredded mozzarella cheese

Preheat the oven to 400°F. In a large skillet, over medium-high heat, fry the sausage for about 5 minutes, or until no pink remains; drain. Remove from the heat, then mix in the tomato paste, tomato sauce, mushrooms, garlic, oregano, salt, and pepper. Place the bread halves on a lightly greased cookie sheet. Spread the sausage mixture evenly on the bread; top with cheese. Bake for 15 to 20 minutes, or until the cheese is melted and starts to brown.

NOTE: If you're using Italian turkey sausage, you may need to add 1 to 2 tablespoons vegetable oil to the skillet. This is great made ahead and baked just before serving—and it even freezes well, uncooked (bake just before serving)! For an added treat, top with hot or sweet pepper rings or sliced ripe olives.

creamy tomato chicken spread

about 3 cups

We're always looking for new things to serve our company.
Here's a great party treat that's a little different from the rest.

1 teaspoon vegetable oil	1 teaspoon sugar
1 pound ground chicken or turkey	¾ teaspoon dried oregano
½ cup chopped onion	1 teaspoon chili powder
1 garlic clove, minced	1 package (8 ounces) cream cheese, softened
1 can (8 ounces) tomato sauce	⅓ cup grated Parmesan cheese
¼ cup ketchup	

In a large skillet, heat the oil over medium-high heat. Add the chicken, onion, and garlic; cook, stirring, until the chicken is brown and the onion is tender, about 5 minutes. Add the tomato sauce, ketchup, sugar, oregano, and chili powder; stir well, then reduce heat to low and simmer, covered, for about 10 minutes. Add the cheeses; stir and cook on low until the cheese is melted, about 5 minutes. Serve warm.

NOTE: Serve with warmed tortilla chips for dipping. . . . Mmmm!! This is a great make-ahead—just store it in the refrigerator and rewarm before serving.

turkey stuffed mushrooms

about 40 stuffed mushrooms
(about 2¼ cups stuffing)

*Stuffed mushrooms . . . everybody loves 'em! (And the best part
is you get so many with so little work.)*

1	tablespoon vegetable oil	1	teaspoon dried dillweed
1	pound turkey breakfast sausage	2 to 3	tablespoons chopped scallions
1	package (8 ounces) cream cheese, softened	3	pounds stuffing mushrooms, cleaned and stems removed (about 40)
½	teaspoon salt		Seasoned bread crumbs for sprinkling
¼	teaspoon pepper		

Preheat the oven to 400°F. In a large skillet, heat the oil over medium-high heat; brown the sausage, stirring to break up, and drain off excess liquid. In a medium-sized bowl, mix the browned sausage with the cream cheese, salt, pepper, dillweed, and scallions. Stuff the mushrooms with the sausage mixture, place on cookie sheets that have been coated with nonstick vegetable spray, sprinkle with bread crumbs, and bake for 25 minutes or until lightly browned. Transfer to a serving platter and serve warm.

greek spinach soup

6 cups

Here's a different way to enjoy great results from basic chicken broth. It makes you feel warm all over (just like the sunny Mediterranean beaches of Greece)!

1 can (15 ounces) chick peas, drained well

6 cups chicken broth

1 box (10 ounces) frozen chopped spinach, thawed and drained

⅓ cup olive oil

4 garlic cloves, minced

2 teaspoons finely chopped fresh parsley

Juice of 1 lemon

Croutons for topping

Place the chick peas and broth in a large pot; simmer over a low heat for 10 minutes. Add the spinach, olive oil, garlic, parsley, and lemon juice and simmer for 10 minutes more. Raise the heat to high and bring the soup to a quick boil. Pour the soup into a large serving bowl, stir, top with croutons, and serve.

garlic soup

about 4 cups

*This Spanish soup gives you another way to surprise
everybody —with that ever-popular flavor: garlic!*

4 to 5 garlic cloves, peeled and
    slightly crushed

2 tablespoons olive oil

1 quart (4 cups) chicken stock
    or broth

¼ teaspoon salt

¼ teaspoon pepper

2 slices stale bread, cut into
    cubes

1 egg, beaten

In a soup pot, over medium-high heat, sauté the garlic in the
olive oil until golden. Remove from the heat and cool slightly. Return the pot to a low heat and slowly add stock, salt, pepper, and
bread. Simmer for 2 to 3 minutes. Remove 2 tablespoons of the
soup broth and mix with the egg. Add the egg mixture to the soup
and stir. Continue cooking until the soup starts to thicken, about
2 minutes. Serve.

NOTE: If you don't have any stale bread, this works just as well
with toast or croutons.

parsnip and spinach cream soup

about 9 cups

Wait till you taste this creamy combination of parsnips and spinach.
It's so different that even the non–spinach lovers will love it!

1¼	quarts chicken broth	5	ounces (½ of a 10-ounce
1½	pounds fresh parsnips,		bag) fresh spinach
	peeled and cut into ¼-inch	¼	cup Dijon mustard
	slices	1½	cups heavy cream or half-
1	medium-sized onion, thinly		and-half
	sliced	½	teaspoon pepper
1	celery stalk, thinly sliced		

Place the chicken broth in a soup pot, then add the parsnips, onion, and celery, and cook over medium-high heat. Bring to a boil, then lower the heat to medium and cook for 20 to 30 minutes, or until the vegetables are tender. Remove the pot from the heat and stir in the spinach. Pour the mixture into a blender or food processor and purée until smooth; return the mixture to the pot. Stir in the mustard, cream, and pepper.

NOTE: Serve hot or chilled.

marinades, sauces, and other light 'n' easies

SPARKLY MARINADES   43
Poultry Marinade   43
Garlic and Hot Pepper Marinade   43
Delicate and Fancy Marinade   44

LEMON COAT CHICKEN   45

GARLICKY BAKED CHICKEN   46

BALSAMIC MARINATED CHICKEN   47

SPICY CHICKEN   48

GRILLED CHICKABOB   49

CHICKEN TERIYAKI   50

SLICED TURKEY SPREAD   51

TOMATO-BASIL TURKEY SAUCE   52

TURKEY MACARONI SALAD   53

MEDITERRANEAN TURKEY SALAD   54

NEW POTATO SALAD WITH TURKEY   55

sparkly marinades

*Whether you're broiling, grilling, or baking, marinades add
an extra-special flavor and moistness you'll love.
Here are a few of my favorites:*

poultry marinade

about ⅔ cup

(enough for 1 to 2 pounds boneless chicken breasts)

½ cup vegetable oil

¼ cup lemon juice

2 garlic cloves, minced

1 tablespoon chicken-flavored instant bouillon

1½ teaspoons thyme leaves

Mix together all the ingredients in a medium-sized bowl. Use immediately or store in a covered container in the refrigerator until ready to use.

NOTE: Use as a marinade for chicken or turkey breasts, or chicken pieces. Marinate in the refrigerator, covered, for up to 1 hour, turning occasionally, then cook as desired.

garlic and hot pepper marinade

about 1 cup

(enough for 1 to 2 pounds boneless chicken breasts)

¾ cup vegetable oil

⅓ cup lemon juice

2 tablespoons chopped jalapeño peppers

1 tablespoon chicken-flavored instant bouillon

2 teaspoons ground ginger

2 garlic cloves, minced

2 teaspoons thyme leaves

Mix together all the ingredients in a medium-sized bowl. Use immediately or store in a covered container in the refrigerator until ready to use.

NOTE: Use as a marinade for chicken or turkey breasts. Marinate in the refrigerator, covered, for up to 1 hour, turning occasionally, then cook as desired.

43

delicate and fancy marinade

1 cup marinade

(enough for 2 boneless chicken breasts)

Delicate and fancy-tasting, yes, but so easy to make, too.

2 tablespoons white vinegar

1 garlic clove, minced

1 tablespoon Dijon-style mustard

¼ teaspoon dried parsley

¼ teaspoon thyme leaves

¼ teaspoon marjoram

¾ cup olive oil

¼ teaspoon pepper

In a small bowl, mix together the vinegar, garlic, mustard, parsley, thyme, and marjoram. Whisk in the olive oil and pepper. Use immediately or store in the refrigerator, covered, until ready to use.

NOTE: Allow 2 chicken breasts to marinate in this mixture in the refrigerator, covered, for 30 minutes. This also works well with fish or beef (but let beef sit in the marinade for an extra 15 minutes).

lemon coat chicken

4 to 6 servings

(makes about 1 cup marinade)

We're all caught up in life's hustle and bustle, but we still want to say, "I made this myself." Here's a way to put that homemade goodness on your table without spending a lot of time in the kitchen.

MARINADE

½ cup Dijon-style mustard

¼ cup vegetable oil

¼ cup lemon juice

½ teaspoon dried dillweed

4 chicken breasts, split, skinned, and boned

Combine all the marinade ingredients in a large bowl. Add the chicken breasts and coat completely. Cover and refrigerate for about 1 hour. After marinating, preheat the oven to broil and place the chicken on a broiler pan; discard excess marinade. Broil the chicken for 5 to 7 minutes per side, or until fork-tender and no pink remains.

NOTE: Why not try a different flavoring each time you make it—maybe basil one time and tarragon, cumin, curry, or chili powder the next? (It's great cooked on the grill, too!)

garlicky baked chicken

3 to 4 servings

What garlic goodness—I love it!
(Yes, I think you'll still get kissed!)

MARINADE

½ cup mayonnaise

⅛ cup Italian dressing

¼ teaspoon garlic powder

¼ teaspoon Italian seasoning

½ teaspoon brown seasoning
sauce

2 chicken breasts, split,
skinned, and boned

Chopped fresh parsley for
garnish

In a medium-sized bowl, mix together all the marinade ingredients. Place the chicken in the marinade, cover, and marinate in the refrigerator for 20 minutes. Preheat the oven to 350°F. Shake off the marinade from the chicken, discard excess marinade, and place the chicken in a baking pan that has been coated with non-stick vegetable spray. Bake for about 15 minutes, or until the chicken is fork-tender and no pink remains. Sprinkle with parsley before serving.

NOTE: This is great grilled or broiled, too.

balsamic marinated chicken

3 to 4 servings

The balsamic vinegar gives the chicken such a nice taste!
It's liable to become one of your family's
favorites, like it did mine.

MARINADE

½ cup balsamic vinegar

¼ cup olive oil

½ teaspoon garlic powder

¼ teaspoon pepper

2 chicken breasts, split, skinned, and boned

In a large bowl, combine the marinade ingredients. Add the chicken, cover, and marinate in refrigerator for up to ½ hour. Remove the chicken from the marinade, discard the excess marinade, and grill for 8 to 10 minutes per side, or until the chicken is fork-tender and no pink remains. Serve hot or cold.

NOTE: If you want to serve this cold, cut the chicken into chunks and place over salad greens.

spicy chicken

3 to 4 servings

*This sure wakes up drowsy taste buds. Plus, it's great
'cause spicy is very "in" right now.
And it's easy. . . . And that's always "in"!*

MARINADE
½ cup olive oil
½ cup lemon juice
2 teaspoons crushed red
   pepper
¼ teaspoon black pepper

2 chicken breast, split,
   skinned, and boned

In a large bowl, whisk together the marinade ingredients. Add the chicken breast halves and turn to coat thoroughly. Cover the bowl and marinate in refrigerator for up to 1 hour, turning the breasts occasionally. Preheat oven to broil. Remove the chicken from the marinade, discard excess marinade, place on a broiler pan, and broil for 6 to 8 minutes. Turn the chicken and broil for 5 to 10 minutes more, or until it is fork-tender and no pink remains.

grilled chickabob

3 to 4 servings
(about 2 cups marinade)

A different way to serve chicken that's tasty, easy, and fun!
They'll love the taste, and the name, too.

MARINADE

¾ cup soy sauce

¾ cup apricot preserves or orange marmalade

2 tablespoons white vinegar

2 tablespoons peanut or vegetable oil

2 tablespoons brown sugar

1 teaspoon garlic powder

¼ teaspoon hot pepper sauce

2 chicken breasts, split, skinned, and boned

In a large bowl, whisk together all the marinade ingredients. Remove the fillet from the bottom of each chicken breast half; take out the tough white tendon. Cut each chicken breast piece in half lengthwise (do not cut the fillets). (There should be a total of 12 pieces of chicken.) Add the chicken pieces to the marinade, cover, and marinate in the refrigerator for up to ½ hour. Heat a grill to medium-high heat. Skewer the marinated chicken pieces like a ribbon, and grill until the chicken is done and no pink remains.

NOTE: For a complete and delicious meal, serve with grilled vegetables over hot cooked rice.

chicken teriyaki

6 to 8 servings

*Whether you're grilling or broiling, here's a way to zest up
your chicken. The marinade does all the flavoring.*

MARINADE
½ cup soy sauce
¼ cup firmly packed brown
  sugar
2 tablespoons vegetable oil
1 teaspoon ground ginger
¼ teaspoon pepper
2 garlic cloves, minced

4 chicken breasts, split,
  skinned, and boned

In a large bowl, mix together the marinade ingredients. Add the
chicken breasts, cover, and marinate for up to ½ hour in the refrigerator. When ready to cook, heat the oven to broil, remove the
chicken to a broiler pan, discarding excess marinade. Broil the
chicken for 5 to 7 minutes per side, or until the chicken is fork-
tender and no pink remains.

marinades, sauces, and others

sliced turkey spread

⅔ cup

*Here's an especially simple way to take a turkey sandwich
and turn it into "simply special."*

⅓ cup mayonnaise

⅓ cup grated Parmesan cheese

1 teaspoon dried chives

1 teaspoon crushed fresh or
  bottled garlic

In a medium-sized bowl, combine all the ingredients. Cover and store in the refrigerator until ready to use.

NOTE: Try serving it like this: Slice French bread in half lengthwise, place the turkey and tomato slices over both bread halves, cover with the spread, and broil until warm and golden. Slice and enjoy!

tomato-basil turkey sauce

about 1⅔ cups

*Perk up plain sliced turkey with this sauce
for a nice change.*

½ cup mayonnaise

½ cup milk

¼ teaspoon dried basil

1 small tomato, finely chopped

1 scallion, finely chopped

In a medium-sized saucepan, combine the mayonnaise, milk, and basil. Cook over medium heat, stirring, until the mixture thickens and begins to boil. Stir in the tomato and scallion. Serve hot or cold.

NOTE: This is great served over sliced, cooked turkey. Try fresh basil instead of the dried, or for a different taste treat, try fresh dill. Light mayonnaise will also work well.

turkey macaroni salad

about 12 servings

*Any extras you add in will make this a picnic or potluck
favorite that's just a little more special.
Make enough for seconds!*

1 pound elbow macaroni	4 cups cooked turkey chunks
6 hard-boiled eggs, chopped	1 teaspoon salt
1 cup chopped celery	1 teaspoon pepper
2 cups mayonnaise	

In a large pot of boiling water, cook the macaroni just until tender; drain, cool, and place in a large bowl. Add the remaining ingredients and mix together. Serve immediately or refrigerate until ready to serve.

NOTE: If making this in advance, you may need to add extra mayonnaise before serving. For a different taste treat you may want to add ½ teaspoon celery seed, or 1 teaspoon dried dillweed or basil.

mediterranean turkey salad

3 to 4 servings

Wow! With ethnic flavors being so popular . . . Mmm! Mmm!

½ cup olive oil, divided

4 turkey cutlets (about 1 pound)

3 scallions, sliced

¼ teaspoon pepper

3 tablespoons wine vinegar, divided

1 teaspoon Dijon-style mustard

2 tablespoons mayonnaise

1 cup cherry tomatoes, cut in half

½ cup black olives, rinsed

2 tablespoons chopped fresh parsley

In a large skillet, heat 2 tablespoons of the oil over medium-high heat; add the turkey cutlets and sauté until lightly browned and no pink remains, about 5 minutes on each side. Cool and cut into cubes. In a large bowl, combine the turkey cubes with the scallions and sprinkle with pepper. In a small bowl, mix 2 tablespoons of the olive oil and 1 tablespoon of the wine vinegar; stir into the turkey mixture and marinate, covered, for 15 minutes in the refrigerator. Meanwhile, in a small bowl, whisk together the mustard, mayonnaise, and remaining oil and vinegar. Pour the mustard-mayonnaise mixture over the marinated turkey and stir. Add the cherry tomatoes, olives, and parsley; toss.

NOTE: Serve over romaine lettuce leaves.

new potato salad with turkey

12 to 16 servings

*Here's a new hearty twist on a popular picnic and potluck
supper dish. Whatever the occasion, you'll be a hit!*

6 pounds cleaned red or white new baby or regular potatoes	2 pounds smoked turkey breast, cut into bite-sized pieces
DRESSING	1 cup chopped celery
1½ cups mayonnaise	1 cup chopped red bell pepper
1½ cups sour cream	1 cup chopped scallion
½ cup prepared mustard	
½ cup chopped fresh parsley	
1 teaspoon salt	
Pepper to taste	

Put the potatoes (with skins on) in a large pot, add enough
water to cover, and boil for 18 to 20 minutes, or until tender. Meanwhile, in a large bowl, combine all the dressing ingredients; mix
well and set aside. Drain the cooked potatoes and cool slightly,
then cut into quarters and place in a large bowl. (If using regular
potatoes, cut them into sixths or eighths.) Add the smoked turkey,
celery, red pepper, and scallion. Pour the dressing over the potato
mixture and chill for about 2 hours or even overnight to "marry"
the flavors, stirring occasionally.

NOTE: This is especially nice served garnished with fresh herbs.
This recipe can easily be cut in half to make a smaller portion.

main courses

ALMOST-FRIED CHICKEN   61

EASY SWEET 'N' SOUR CHICKEN   62

POULET MARENGO   63

CRANBERRY CHICKEN   64

CHICKEN WITH LEMON SAUCE   65

LOUISIANA CHICKEN   66

CHINESE CHICKEN   67

FRENCH COUNTRY CHICKEN   68

CRISPY PARMESAN CHICKEN   69

SWEET 'N' SOUR TENDERS   70

GARLIC ROASTED CHICKEN   71

CHICKEN ITALIAN   72

"DON'T PEEK" CHICKEN   73

CHICKEN EASY   74

CHICKEN DIVAN   75

CHICKEN IN WINE SAUCE   76

HERBED 'N' SPICED CHICKEN   77

CHICKEN "NORMAND-Y"   78

CHICKEN IN TOMATO MARSALA SAUCE   79

COUNTRY GOODNESS CHICKEN   80

CHICKEN "FANCEE"   81

SIMPLY GOOD CHICKEN   82

DIJON CHICKEN BREASTS   83

BISTRO CHICKEN   84

LIGHT LEMON-DILL CHICKEN   85

GARLIC CHICKEN FLORENTINE   86

GLAZED CHICKEN BREASTS   87

CHEESY BAKED CHICKEN   88

CRISPY-COAT CHICKEN   89

IMPOSSIBLE CHICKEN 'N' BROCCOLI PIE   90

TURKEY OSCAR   91

ITALIAN BAKED CUTLETS   92

TURKEY MUSHROOM MEAT LOAF   93

TURKEY MEAT LOAF FLORENTINE   94

LIGHTER BURGERS   95

TURKEY "POT ROAST"   96

TACO TURKEY   97

CAJUN TURKEY   98

SUPER BOWL TURKEY STRIPS   99

TURKEY "EVERYTHING"   100

TURKEY HASH CAKES   101

BUFFALO-STYLE TURKEY WINGS   102

"one-pans" 103

CHICKEN RATATOUILLE 105

TARRAGON CHICKEN BREAST 106

CHICKEN AND SAUSAGE 107

CURRY CHICKEN 108

CHICKEN WITH SUMMER VEGETABLES 109

ITALIAN CHICKEN AND RICE 110

SKILLET CHICKEN 111

CHICKEN WITH ZUCCHINI AND TOMATOES 112

FRENCH CHICKEN BREASTS IN WINE SAUCE 113

SAUSAGE AND CHICKEN LIVERS 114

COMPANY STEW 115

BLACK-EYED PEA SKILLET 116

TWO-BEAN TURKEY CHILI 117

CHUCK WAGON MIX 118

taste adventures   119

HONEY CHICKEN   121

ROAST CHICKEN AND KIWI WITH
RASPBERRY GLAZE   122

THAI CHICKEN   123

CHICKEN EGG FOO-YUNG   124

CHICKEN FRIED RICE   125

NUTTY DRUMMERS   126

CHICKEN BREASTS WITH BALSAMIC VINEGAR   127

CHICKEN AVOCADO MELT   128

NORTH AFRICAN CHICKEN   129

PROVOLONE CHICKEN   130

ROAST CHICKEN WITH CURRIED HONEY
MUSTARD SAUCE   131

CHICKEN WITH APPLE SALSA   132

RANCH CHICKEN BREASTS   133

PEPPERED RASPBERRY CHICKEN   134

almost-fried chicken

3 to 4 servings

*If you're staying away from a lot of "fried" . . . here's an oven
version that has fried taste without all the fat.*

½ cup all-purpose flour

¼ cup cornmeal

½ teaspoon pepper

½ teaspoon paprika

½ teaspoon garlic powder

½ teaspoon onion powder

2 chicken breasts, split,
  skinned, and boned

¼ cup olive oil

Preheat the oven to 350°F. Pour the flour, cornmeal, pepper, paprika, garlic powder, and onion powder into a paper bag or shallow dish. Place the chicken breasts in the bag and shake until coated, or place in a shallow dish, turning to coat. Place the coated chicken breasts in a baking pan and pour the olive oil over them. Bake for about 45 minutes, or until the chicken is golden and no pink remains, turning several times.

easy sweet 'n' sour chicken

4 to 6 servings

*Here's the easiest sweet 'n' sour you'll ever find!
Tastiest, too.*

1 bottle (8 ounces) Russian
dressing

1 package onion soup mix
(from a 2-ounce box)

1 jar (12 ounces) apricot
preserves

3 chicken breasts, split,
skinned, and boned

Preheat the oven to 350°F. In a medium-sized bowl, mix together the dressing, preserves, and onion soup. Place the chicken in a 9" × 13" baking pan; pour the dressing mixture over the chicken. Bake for 25 minutes, covered, then uncover and bake for 20 minutes more, or until the chicken is fork-tender and no pink remains.

NOTE: Serve over hot cooked rice.

poulet marengo

4 to 6 servings

This is definitely fancy for company and easy for you.
Exotic-sounding, isn't it?

½ cup all-purpose flour

2 teaspoons salt

½ teaspoon pepper

1 teaspoon dried basil

3 chicken breasts, split, skinned, and boned

¼ cup vegetable oil

¼ cup (½ stick) butter or margarine

1 cup dry white wine

12 ounces mushrooms, sliced

2 garlic cloves, chopped (or to taste)

½ teaspoon sugar

1 can (28 ounces) whole tomatoes, undrained and broken up

1 tablespoon chopped fresh parsley

Preheat the oven to 350°F. In a shallow bowl, mix together the flour, salt, pepper, and basil. Coat the chicken with the flour mixture; reserve remaining flour mixture. In a large skillet, heat the oil and butter over medium heat; sauté the chicken until light golden. Remove the chicken from the skillet and place in a 9" × 13" glass baking dish. Reduce heat to low, then add the remaining flour mixture to the oil and butter in the skillet; stir until well blended. Add the wine, a little at a time, stirring with a whisk or spoon until smooth and thick. Add the mushrooms, garlic, sugar, and tomatoes, stirring. Pour the mixture over the chicken, cover, and bake for 40 to 50 minutes, or until the chicken is fork-tender and no pink remains. Sprinkle with parsley and serve.

NOTE: I like this served over pasta with the sauce from the pan.

63

cranberry chicken

3 to 4 servings

*A prizewinner that teams foods that were meant for each
other. And don't let the cranberry sauce make you think it's
only for autumn. . . . Uh! Uh! It's a unique,
welcome taste all year long.*

¼ cup vegetable oil

1 chicken (2½ to 3 pounds),
cut into 8 pieces

¼ teaspoon salt

¼ teaspoon pepper

½ cup chopped onion

¼ cup chopped celery

1 can (16 ounces) whole-berry
cranberry sauce

½ cup ketchup

2 tablespoons lemon juice

1 tablespoon brown sugar

1 tablespoon Worcestershire
sauce

1 tablespoon prepared
mustard

1 tablespoon white vinegar

Preheat the oven to 350°F. In a large skillet, heat the oil over
medium-high heat; sprinkle the chicken with salt and pepper, then
add to the skillet and brown. Remove the chicken and place in a
9" × 13" baking pan that has been coated with nonstick vegetable
spray. In the same skillet, cook the onion and celery until tender
(do not brown). Skim off excess fat and discard. Stir in the remaining ingredients; heat through. Pour the mixture over the
chicken. Bake, uncovered, for about 50 minutes, or until the
chicken is done and no pink remains, basting 2 or 3 times during
baking.

chicken with lemon sauce

4 to 6 servings

Sometimes we want to get away from heavy flavors and have something with a light, crisp taste. Here's the answer!

½ cup dry bread crumbs

3 chicken breasts, split, skinned, and boned

½ cup mayonnaise, divided

4 tablespoons margarine, divided

½ cup chopped onion

3 tablespoons all-purpose flour

1½ cups chicken broth

¼ cup chopped fresh parsley

3 tablespoons lemon juice

Place the bread crumbs in a shallow dish; set aside. Brush the chicken pieces with ¼ cup of the mayonnaise; dip in the bread crumbs to coat. In a large skillet, melt 2 tablespoons of the margarine over medium heat; add the chicken and cook for 15 minutes, turning occasionally, or until golden and done. Remove to a serving platter and keep warm. In a medium-sized saucepan, heat the remaining 2 tablespoons margarine over medium heat; add the onion and sauté until transparent. Stir in the flour until well blended. Gradually stir in the broth. Add the parsley and lemon juice. Cook, stirring, until the mixture boils. Add the remaining ¼ cup mayonnaise; cook, stirring, until hot. Spoon the mixture over the chicken and serve.

louisiana chicken

6 to 8 servings

Chicken and gravy all in one dish. And some extra zip (you know, hot pepper sauce) makes it Louisiana-style cooking at its best.

¼ to ½ cup vegetable oil

2 chickens (2½ to 3 pounds each), each cut into 8 pieces

½ cup all-purpose flour

4 medium-sized celery stalks, thinly sliced

3 medium-sized green bell peppers, cut into thin strips

2 medium-sized onions, diced

3 cups chicken broth

2¼ teaspoons salt

½ teaspoon hot pepper sauce

Preheat the oven to 350°F. In a large skillet, heat ¼ cup oil over medium-high heat; cook the chicken, a few pieces at a time, until browned on all sides, adding additional oil as needed. Remove the browned chicken to two 9" × 13" baking pans that have been coated with nonstick vegetable spray, dividing the pieces evenly between the 2 pans; set aside. Add the flour to the skillet juices and cook over medium heat for 30 seconds or less, stirring constantly, until the flour is golden. Add the celery, green peppers, and onions; cook for about 5 minutes, or until the vegetables are tender, stirring frequently. Stir in the broth, salt, and hot pepper sauce. Bring the mixture to a boil, then pour over the chicken, dividing it evenly between the two pans. Bake, uncovered, for 50 to 60 minutes, or until the chicken is fork-tender and no pink remains, basting occasionally.

NOTE: You can easily cut this recipe in half, but for the same work, why not make it all and freeze the leftovers for a later date—it'll taste just as good!! Serve over hot cooked rice.

main courses

chinese chicken

3 to 4 servings

This will be a family favorite 'cause it tastes so good, and it'll be your favorite 'cause it goes together in a snap!

1 chicken (2½ to 3 pounds), cut into 8 pieces	¼ cup white vinegar
⅓ cup soy sauce	1 garlic clove, crushed
	2 tablespoons cornstarch

Place all the ingredients, except the cornstarch, in a Dutch oven and simmer, covered, for 60 to 70 minutes, or until chicken is done, turning occasionally. Remove the chicken to a serving platter; keep warm. Remove ¼ cup of the pan juices from the Dutch oven and pour into a small saucepan, bring to a boil, add the cornstarch and stir until thickened, about 1 to 2 minutes. Pour over the chicken and serve.

NOTE: Serve over hot cooked rice.

french country chicken

about 4 servings

When we hear "French," we usually think fancy. Well, that's not always so. Here's a country-style dish that's cooked in one pot—right! Like we'd get in a family restaurant in the French countryside.

2 tablespoons olive or vegetable oil

1 chicken (2½ to 3 pounds), cut into 8 pieces

1 envelope onion soup mix (from a 2-ounce box)

2 cups water

¼ cup sherry

2 tablespoons Dijon-style mustard

1 package (8 to 9 ounces) frozen snap peas, thawed

1 package (10 ounces) frozen sliced carrots, thawed

2 tablespoons all-purpose flour

1 cup (½ pint) sour cream

Heat the oil over medium-high heat in a large skillet. Add the chicken and brown; drain off the oil. In a small bowl, combine the onion soup mix, water, sherry, and mustard. Add to the skillet and bring to a boil; reduce the heat and simmer, covered, for 20 minutes. Stir in the peas and carrots and cook for another 10 to 15 minutes. Remove the chicken and vegetables to a serving platter and keep warm; reserve the liquid in the skillet. Boil reserved liquid over high heat for about 8 minutes, then remove it from the heat. In a small bowl, combine the flour and sour cream; stir into the skillet mixture and return to a low heat. Bring just to the boiling point, then reduce heat and simmer, stirring constantly, just until sauce is thickened, about 3 minutes. Pour the sauce over the chicken and vegetables and serve.

NOTE: Serve it with some nice crusty bread to soak up the creamy sauce.... Mmmm!!

crispy parmesan chicken

about 4 servings

Here's a way to get the great taste of frying . . . in baking!
There's less fat, but still plenty of flavor,
'cause it's in the coating.

1 envelope (about 1½ ounces) dry spaghetti sauce mix

1⅓ cups dry bread crumbs

⅓ cup grated Parmesan cheese

1 can (8 ounces) tomato sauce

1 chicken (2½ to 3 pounds), cut into 8 pieces

2 tablespoons vegetable oil

Preheat the oven to 400°F. In a small bowl, combine the spaghetti sauce mix, bread crumbs, and cheese. Pour tomato sauce into another small bowl. Dip the chicken pieces into the tomato sauce, then into the bread crumb mixture. Place the chicken in a foil-lined 9" × 13" baking pan and drizzle with the vegetable oil. Bake for 50 to 55 minutes, or until chicken is fork-tender and no pink remains.

sweet 'n' sour tenders

3 to 4 servings

*These wonderful flavor combinations are sure to please your family.
(Every so often you'll find sales on the chicken tenderloins,
and when you do, grab them! They're
white meat at its best.)*

1 tablespoon vegetable oil

2 chicken breasts, skinned, boned, and cut into strips

1 package (⅞ ounce) sweet-and-sour sauce mix or 3 tablespoons sweet-and-sour sauce mix

1 can (20 ounces) pineapple chunks in syrup, drained (reserve syrup)

¼ cup water

1 tablespoon sugar

1 teaspoon white vinegar

¼ cup ketchup

1 medium-sized green bell pepper, cut into strips

In a large skillet, heat the oil over medium-high heat; add the chicken and cook for 5 to 6 minutes, or until browned on both sides. In a small bowl, combine the sweet-and-sour sauce mix, reserved pineapple syrup, water, sugar, vinegar, and ketchup. Pour over the chicken. Add the pineapple and green pepper. Reduce heat to low and cook, covered, for 10 to 12 minutes, or until heated through.

NOTE: Serve over hot cooked rice.

garlic roasted chicken

3 to 4 servings

If you like garlic (and even if you don't), you'll love this!
It's just loaded with great taste. It's not a heavy garlic
taste, though, 'cause the cooking mellows out
the sharpness and leaves a full smoothness.

1   chicken (2½ to 3 pounds),
    cut into 8 pieces
¼ cup olive oil
½ teaspoon salt
½ teaspoon pepper

½ teaspoon dried oregano
½ teaspoon dried basil
1   head of garlic, unpeeled and
    cut crosswise into 3 slices,
    broken up

Preheat the oven to 350°F. Place the chicken in a 9" × 13" baking pan; set aside. In a small bowl, mix together the oil, salt, pepper, oregano, and basil; set aside. Distribute the garlic over the chicken, cover with the oil mixture, distributing evenly over the chicken, and bake for 50 to 60 minutes, or until the chicken is golden and no pink remains, turning occasionally. Discard the garlic before serving.

NOTE: Real garlic lovers can save the garlic—just pop off the skin and serve it with the chicken—wow!!

chicken italian

3 to 4 servings

Here's an easy old-time chicken recipe that's found in almost every Italian kitchen. And, true to form, it's Italian delicious!

2 eggs, well beaten

¼ cup Italian-style seasoned bread crumbs

2 tablespoons grated Parmesan cheese

2 chicken breasts, split, skinned, and boned

¼ cup plus 1 tablespoon olive oil, divided

2 garlic cloves, minced

1 large onion, chopped

½ teaspoon dried basil

½ teaspoon dried oregano

⅛ teaspoon crushed red pepper

Place beaten eggs in a shallow dish. In another shallow dish, combine the bread crumbs and Parmesan cheese. Dip the chicken breasts in egg, then in the bread crumb mixture. In a large skillet, heat the ¼ cup olive oil over medium-high heat; add coated chicken and sauté for 6 to 8 minutes per side, or until the chicken is golden and no pink remains. Remove the chicken and place on a serving platter; keep warm. In the same skillet, heat the remaining 1 tablespoon olive oil; add the remaining ingredients and sauté until garlic and onion are golden. Top the chicken breasts with the garlic-onion mixture and serve.

"don't peek" chicken

about 4 servings

*Let the oven do most of the work while you take care of the
kids, take care of the house, take care of the pets,
take care of the . . . well, you get the idea!*

1 cup uncooked rice

1 can (10¾ ounces) cream of
mushroom soup

1 can (10¾ ounces) cream of
celery soup

1 envelope onion soup mix
(from a 2-ounce box)

1 soup can cold water

1 garlic clove, crushed

1 teaspoon chopped fresh
parsley

1 teaspoon Worcestershire
sauce

1 chicken (3½ to 4 pounds),
cut into 8 pieces

Paprika for sprinkling

Preheat the oven to 350°F. Lightly grease a 9" × 13" baking
pan; set aside. In a large bowl, mix together the rice, three soups,
water, garlic, parsley, and Worcestershire sauce. Pour the mixture
into the baking pan. Press the chicken into the mixture. Sprinkle
the top with paprika, cover tightly with aluminum foil, and bake
for 2½ hours. Do NOT open the cover (not even to peek) during
baking.

NOTE: This is great made ahead and rewarmed in the oven or microwave. For a different taste treat, why not try adding some carrot
or celery chunks or using a flavored rice? And remember, bottled
garlic is a wonderful time-saver.

chicken easy

4 to 5 servings

*Here's an easy way to bring back that yesterday,
cooked-all-day taste in a lot less time, with a lot less work,
but with all the same goodness.*

1 chicken (4 to 5 pounds), cut into 8 pieces

1 can (10¾ ounces) cream of chicken soup

1 tablespoon prepared mustard

½ teaspoon pepper

½ teaspoon onion powder

½ cup water

Place the chicken pieces in a large pot. In a medium-sized bowl, combine the soup, mustard, pepper, onion powder, and water; mix well. Pour the soup mixture over the chicken. Bring to a very slow boil; cover, reduce heat and simmer for 2 hours, stirring occasionally, until the chicken is tender and no pink remains. Serve hot.

NOTE: Serve over hot cooked rice, noodles, pasta, or with bread for dunking. For a different taste treat, try ½ teaspoon of either dill-weed, caraway seed, dried tarragon, or oregano. Fresh celery or carrot chunks are a nice addition, too.

chicken divan

3 to 4 servings

Sounds like an elegant dinner at the Ritz, but it's really so easy. When your company tastes this, they'll think you spent all day in the kitchen, and only you'll need to know the truth.

1 pound fresh broccoli, cut into spears, cooked and drained, or 1 package (10 ounces) frozen broccoli spears, thawed

2 chicken breasts, split, skinned, and boned

3 tablespoons melted butter or margarine, divided

1 can (10¾ ounces) condensed broccoli cheese soup

⅓ cup milk

2 tablespoons dry bread crumbs

Preheat the oven to 400°F. Arrange the broccoli in the bottom of an 8-inch square baking pan that has been coated with nonstick vegetable spray; set aside. In a large skillet over medium heat, brown the chicken in 2 tablespoons butter. Place the browned chicken over the broccoli. In a medium-sized bowl, combine the soup and milk. Pour over the chicken. In a small bowl, combine the remaining 1 tablespoon melted butter with the bread crumbs; sprinkle over the top. Bake for 15 to 20 minutes, or until hot and the chicken is cooked thoroughly.

NOTE: This is even easier with leftover chunked chicken or turkey.

chicken in wine sauce

6 to 8 servings

Whenever I see wine in an ingredient list, I always think "fancy."
Well, the only thing fancy about this recipe is
the taste—the rest is easy!

About ¼ cup all purpose
flour for dredging

4 chicken breasts, split,
skinned, and boned

¼ cup (½ stick) butter or
margarine

SAUCE

2 tablespoons butter or
margarine

1 teaspoon minced garlic

½ teaspoon dried sage

1 teaspoon chopped fresh
parsley

¼ pound mushrooms, sliced

½ cup dry white wine

1 package (10 ounces) frozen
broccoli spears, thawed

Preheat the oven to 350°F. Place the flour in a shallow dish and lightly dredge the chicken in the flour. In a large skillet, melt the ¼ cup butter over medium heat; add the chicken and sauté until golden. Remove the chicken from the skillet and place in a 9" × 13" baking pan that has been coated with nonstick vegetable spray; bake for 10 to 15 minutes, or until the chicken is fork-tender and no pink remains. Meanwhile, add the 2 tablespoons butter to the skillet and sauté the garlic, sage, parsley, and mushrooms for 2 to 3 minutes; add the wine. Using a spatula, scrape together the mushrooms and seasonings. Add the thawed broccoli to the skillet, cover, and let it warm through. Once the chicken is cooked, remove it from the oven and place on a serving platter. Pour the sauce over the chicken and serve immediately.

NOTE: Sometimes I like to add some artichoke hearts or fresh basil to the sauce, if I have any on hand.

herbed 'n' spiced chicken

3 to 4 servings

With all the different ways to prepare chicken, sometimes the basics are best. And here's a basic one with a little twist.

2 cups herb-seasoned stuffing mix

1 chicken (about 3 pounds), cut into 8 pieces

1 teaspoon salt

½ teaspoon pepper

½ cup plain nonfat or low-fat yogurt

Preheat the oven to 350°F. Grease a 9" × 13" baking pan; set aside. Pour the dry stuffing mix into a blender or food processor and process until crumbs form; place the crumbs in a shallow dish. Sprinkle the chicken with salt and pepper, brush with yogurt, then roll in the crumbs. Place the chicken in a single layer, skin side up, in the baking pan and bake for about 55 minutes, or until fork-tender and no pink remains. Serve.

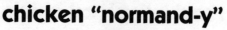

chicken "normand-y"

3 to 4 servings

"Simple but elegant" is a great way to describe this.
It's from the Red Rooster Restaurant in Rhode Island,
so that proves how elegant. Thanks, Normand.

2 eggs	2 whole chicken breasts, split, skinned, boned, and flattened
¼ cup milk	
1 cup cornflake crumbs or finely crushed cornflakes	2 teaspoons olive oil
⅛ teaspoon thyme leaves	2 teaspoons butter

Preheat the oven to 425°F. In a small bowl, beat the eggs and milk; set aside. In a shallow dish, combine the cornflake crumbs with the thyme; set aside. Dip the chicken breast halves in the egg mixture, one at a time, then coat completely with the cornflake crumb mixture. Grease a cookie sheet with the olive oil; lay the chicken breasts on the cookie sheet and dot with butter. Bake for about 15 minutes, or until the chicken is fork-tender and no pink remains.

chicken in tomato marsala sauce

3 to 4 servings

*You just can't beat those great Italian flavorings.
The Marsala wine smooths it out, too, with its
touch of light sweetness. It's a great dish
that you make all in one skillet.*

½ teaspoon dried oregano
¼ teaspoon garlic powder
¼ teaspoon onion powder
¼ teaspoon pepper
2 chicken breasts, split, skinned, and boned
4 ounces fresh mushrooms, sliced
1 can (8 ounces) tomato sauce
¼ cup Marsala wine (medium or sweet)

In a small bowl, combine the oregano, garlic powder, onion powder, and pepper; coat the chicken with the seasonings. Heat a large nonstick skillet over medium heat for about 1 minute, then coat with nonstick vegetable spray. Add the chicken and cook for about 5 minutes. Turn the chicken, add the mushrooms, and cook for 5 minutes more. Push the chicken to the side of the skillet, then add the tomato sauce and wine, stirring together with the mushrooms to mix well. Arrange the chicken in the sauce and simmer for about 12 minutes, or until the chicken is fork-tender and no pink remains.

NOTE: Serve over hot cooked linguine.

country goodness chicken

4 to 6 servings

In my mind, "country-style" means wholesome,
simple, and old-fashioned.
Here's one that goes along with those good ol' values.
One taste, and everybody remembers.

⅓ cup all-purpose flour

3 chicken breasts, skinned, boned, and cut into 1-inch strips

½ to 1 teaspoon salt

¼ teaspoon pepper

¼ to ½ cup vegetable oil (as needed)

1 can (10½ ounces) chicken broth

1 cup hot water

2 tablespoons white wine

⅛ teaspoon marjoram or thyme leaves

Place the flour in a shallow dish; set aside. Sprinkle the chicken strips with salt and pepper; add to the flour, a few strips at a time, and dredge to coat on all sides. In a large skillet, heat ¼ cup oil over medium-high heat. Add the chicken, turning to brown on all sides, and cook for about 10 minutes, adding oil as needed. Pour off excess oil; add the broth and hot water to the skillet. Reduce heat to low, cover, and simmer for 15 minutes. Stir in the wine and marjoram; cover and cook for 5 minutes more, or until the chicken is fork-tender and no pink remains.

NOTE: Serve over biscuits or rice with the sauce from the pan.

chicken "fancee"

3 to 4 servings

*Once in a while we need something a little fancier, a little more
special—maybe for a special guest or a romantic dinner
—but we don't have lots of time. Well, here's a
quick and easy way to get "fancee."*

2 tablespoons butter,
margarine, or olive oil

2 chicken breasts, split,
skinned, and boned

½ cup matchstick-cut carrots

½ cup matchstick-cut zucchini

½ cup sliced mushrooms

1 cup prepared white sauce
(made from a package of
dry mix)

2 tablespoons white wine
(optional)

1 teaspoon Dijon-style
mustard

¼ teaspoon dried rosemary

¼ teaspoon dried tarragon

Dash salt

Dash pepper

2 Australian Toaster® Biscuits
or English muffins, split and
toasted

In a large skillet, melt the butter over medium heat; cook the
chicken until golden and cooked through, about 10 to 15 minutes.
Remove the chicken, set aside, and keep warm. Add the carrots,
zucchini, and mushrooms to the skillet and stir-fry until crisp-
tender, about 1 minute. Stir in the white sauce, wine, mustard,
rosemary, and tarragon. Heat through. Season to taste with salt
and pepper. Diagonally slice the chicken breasts. Arrange the
chicken over the biscuit halves and top with the vegetable sauce.

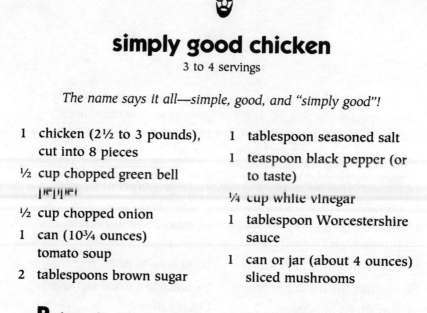

simply good chicken

3 to 4 servings

The name says it all—simple, good, and "simply good"!

- 1 chicken (2½ to 3 pounds), cut into 8 pieces
- ½ cup chopped green bell pepper
- ½ cup chopped onion
- 1 can (10¾ ounces) tomato soup
- 2 tablespoons brown sugar
- 1 tablespoon seasoned salt
- 1 teaspoon black pepper (or to taste)
- ¼ cup white vinegar
- 1 tablespoon Worcestershire sauce
- 1 can or jar (about 4 ounces) sliced mushrooms

Preheat the oven to 325°F. Place the chicken in a 9" × 13" baking pan. In a medium-sized bowl, combine the remaining ingredients; mix well and pour over the chicken. Bake, covered, for 65 to 70 minutes, or until the chicken is fork-tender and no pink remains.

NOTE: Serve over hot cooked rice. If you like the skin to get nice and crispy, you can uncover the pan and turn the oven to broil for the last 5 minutes of cooking.

dijon chicken breasts

3 to 4 servings

Not only upscale and full-flavored, but easy,
quick, and healthy, too!

2 chicken breasts, split,
 skinned, and boned

2 tablespoons Dijon-style
 mustard

1 tablespoon brown sugar

1 tablespoon lemon juice

¼ teaspoon cayenne pepper

¼ teaspoon salt

Preheat the oven to 400°F. Place the chicken in a shallow baking pan in a single layer. In a small bowl, mix together the remaining ingredients. Brush half the mustard mixture over the chicken. Bake for 10 minutes; brush the remaining mixture over the chicken and bake for about 10 minutes more, or until the chicken is fork-tender and no pink remains.

NOTE: Great on the grill, too!

bistro chicken

3 to 4 servings

*Bistro Chicken is the French way of saying this looks fancy,
tastes great, and cooks up in a very short time.*

1	can (10¾ ounces) condensed cream of chicken soup	2	chicken breasts, split, skinned, and boned
½	cup dry white wine	¼	teaspoon black pepper
1	tablespoon Dijon-style mustard		

In a medium-sized bowl, combine the soup, wine, and mustard; set aside. Sprinkle the chicken with pepper; set aside. Coat a large skillet with nonstick vegetable spray, then heat over medium-high heat. Place the chicken in the skillet and cook until lightly browned, turning once. Pour the soup mixture over chicken. Bring to a boil, then reduce heat and simmer for 15 minutes, or until the chicken is fork-tender and no pink remains.

NOTE: Serve the chicken and sauce over hot cooked rice.

light lemon-dill chicken

3 to 4 servings

*Fresh taste with these simple ingredients! Well, look—
lemon, dill, garlic . . . ya' can't miss.*

2	tablespoons olive oil	¼	teaspoon salt
2	tablespoons lemon juice	2	chicken breasts, split, skinned, and boned
2	garlic cloves, crushed		
½	teaspoon dried dillweed		

Preheat the oven to broil. In a small bowl, mix together all the ingredients except the chicken. Place the chicken on a rack in a broiler pan; brush with the olive oil mixture and broil for 6 to 8 minutes. Turn the chicken and broil for 6 to 8 minutes more, or until the chicken is browned and done.

garlic chicken florentine

4 to 6 servings

The flavorings are so subtle. . . . Company
will flip over this!

3   chicken breasts, split,
    skinned, and boned

12 unpeeled and 6 peeled
    garlic cloves

2   packages (10 ounces each)
    frozen chopped spinach,
    thawed and drained well

1   can (10¾ ounces)
    chicken soup

½   cup white wine

1   teaspoon ground ginger

6   slices Swiss cheese

Preheat the oven to 350°F. Place the chicken in a 9" × 13"
baking pan that has been coated with nonstick vegetable spray.
Arrange the unpeeled garlic cloves around the chicken. Spread the
spinach evenly over the top of the chicken. In a blender, combine
the soup, wine, peeled garlic, and ginger; mix until smooth. Pour
the mixture over the chicken, cover, and bake for 1 hour. Top with
cheese slices and bake, uncovered, for 5 minutes more.

glazed chicken breasts

3 to 4 servings

*With our busy schedules, we're always looking for quick and
easy without sacrificing taste. Here's a way to put a
delicious dinner on the table in a snap, even if
you stop at the market on your way home
to pick up the few ingredients.*

1	envelope onion soup mix (from a 2-ounce box)	2	chicken breasts, split, skinned, and boned
⅔	cup apricot preserves	2	large red or green bell peppers, sliced into thin rings
½	cup water		

Preheat the oven to broil. In a small bowl, thoroughly combine the onion soup mix, apricot preserves, and water; set aside. Place the chicken breasts in a foil-lined broiler pan. Top the chicken with the soup mixture and broil for 5 minutes; turn the chicken. Place the pepper rings over the chicken, baste with pan juices, then broil for 5 to 10 minutes more, or until the chicken is fork-tender and no pink remains.

NOTE: Serve over hot cooked rice.

cheesy baked chicken

4 to 6 servings

In search of a new favorite way to prepare chicken? Here it is!
The tasty, easy secret is in the crushed cheese crackers.

1 cup finely crushed cheese crackers	¼ teaspoon cayenne pepper
¼ cup sesame seed	3 chicken breasts, split, skinned, and boned
1 tablespoon chopped fresh parsley	½ cup (1 stick) butter or margarine, melted
½ teaspoon salt	Grated Parmesan cheese for topping (optional)
¼ teaspoon black pepper	

Preheat the oven to 350°F. In a large shallow bowl, combine the cracker crumbs, sesame seed, parsley, salt, and black and cayenne peppers. Dip the chicken in melted butter, then dip in the cracker-crumb mixture. Place the chicken in a baking pan that has been coated with nonstick vegetable spray and bake for 20 to 25 minutes, or until the chicken is golden and no pink remains.

crispy-coat chicken

3 to 4 servings
(4 cups)

We all love breaded chicken, but we don't like the work.
Now enjoy crispy chicken that's easy—and there's
so much you can do to make it your own.

1 bag (7 ounces) herb-style or corn bread stuffing, finely crushed (one 7-ounce bag equals 4 cups stuffing or 2 cups crushed stuffing)

1 package (0.7 ounces) Italian salad dressing mix

2 eggs, well beaten

1 chicken (about 3 pounds), cut into 8 pieces

Preheat the oven to 350°F. In a shallow dish, combine the stuffing crumbs and the Italian dressing mix; set aside. Place the eggs in a large bowl; add the chicken and coat well. Roll the chicken in the crumb mixture, one piece at a time, and coat thoroughly. Place the chicken in a 9" × 13" baking pan that has been coated with nonstick vegetable spray and bake for 1 hour, or until the chicken is fork-tender and no pink remains.

NOTE: For flavor variations, add these ingredients to the stuffing crumbs: Oriental: 1 tablespoon brown sugar, ½ teaspoon ground ginger, and 1 tablespoon sesame seed; Cajun: 2 teaspoons paprika, ½ teaspoon thyme leaves, and 1 teaspoon cayenne pepper; Parmesan: ½ cup grated Parmesan cheese.

impossible chicken 'n' broccoli pie

about 6 servings

Impossible? How 'bout impossibly good and easy!
This is another of those
"throw-it-in-a-pie-plate-and-it-forms-its-own-crust"
pies—which makes it a pleasure for us.

1	package (10 ounces) frozen chopped broccoli, thawed and well drained	⅓	cup chopped onion
		1⅓	cups milk
3	cups (12 ounces) shredded Cheddar cheese, divided	3	eggs
		¾	cup biscuit baking mix
1½	cups cut-up cooked chicken	¾	teaspoon salt
		¼	teaspoon pepper

Preheat the oven to 400°F. Grease a 10-inch deep-dish pie plate. Mix the broccoli, 2 cups of the cheese, chicken, and onion in the pie plate. In a medium-sized bowl, beat the milk, eggs, biscuit baking mix, salt, and pepper until smooth. Pour into the pie plate. Bake for 25 to 35 minutes, or until a knife inserted in the center comes out clean. Top with remaining cheese and bake for 1 to 2 minutes longer, or just until cheese is melted. Let stand for 5 minutes before cutting.

turkey oscar

6 servings

This has the fancy appeal of Veal Oscar, but takes lots less $$!

2 eggs, beaten

2 tablespoons water

1 cup dry bread crumbs

¼ teaspoon salt

¼ teaspoon pepper

6 turkey cutlets, sliced about ⅓-inch thick

½ cup vegetable oil

1 box (9 ounces) asparagus cuts, thawed

½ pound flaked crabmeat or 1 package (8 ounces) imitation crabmeat, flaked

1 package (1¼ ounces) Béarnaise or Hollandaise sauce, prepared according to package directions

Preheat the oven to 375°F. In a shallow dish, beat together the egg and water. In another shallow dish, mix together the bread crumbs, salt, and pepper. Dip the turkey in the egg mixture, then in the bread crumb mixture. In a large skillet, heat the oil over medium-high heat; add the turkey and sauté until golden. Place the cooked turkey in a 9" × 13" baking pan, place the asparagus cuts over the turkey, place the crabmeat over the asparagus, and spoon the Béarnaise sauce over the crabmeat, distributing all evenly. Bake for about 20 minutes, or until the sauce bubbles.

italian baked cutlets

about 12 servings

Didn't think our favorite cutlet recipes could get any better?
Try this one for "better," "easier," and more "today."

1 cup dry bread crumbs	1 cup Italian dressing
¾ cup grated Parmesan cheese	3 pounds turkey cutlets or flattened boneless chicken breasts
¾ cup chopped fresh parsley	
½ teaspoon garlic powder	

Preheat the oven to 325°F. In a large bowl, combine the bread crumbs, Parmesan cheese, parsley, and garlic powder; mix thoroughly. Pour the Italian dressing into a shallow dish; dip the cutlets in the dressing, then in the bread crumb mixture, until well coated. Place the coated cutlets on a cookie sheet and place in the freezer for 1 hour. Coat a baking pan with nonstick vegetable spray; arrange the cutlets on the baking pan and bake for 35 minutes, or until done.

NOTE: One way to cut down on calories is to use a light or reduced-calorie Italian dressing.

turkey mushroom meat loaf

4 to 5 servings

*Meat loaf sure is popular, so here's a way to
enjoy it in a lower-fat version.*

3 tablespoons peanut or vegetable oil

1 large onion, chopped

1 large celery stalk, finely chopped

1 garlic clove, finely chopped (optional)

6 ounces fresh mushrooms, cut into quarters (about 2 cups)

1 pound ground turkey

2 cups seasoned stuffing cubes

2 tablespoons ketchup

1 egg

1 cup chicken bouillon, dissolved in 1 cup hot water, divided

½ teaspoon salt

¼ teaspoon pepper

Preheat the oven to 325°F. Heat the oil over medium heat in a large skillet. Add the onion, celery, and garlic and cook until vegetables are soft and transparent, about 5 minutes. Turn the heat to high, add the mushrooms, and cook for another 3 minutes; place the mixture in a large bowl. Add the ground turkey, stuffing cubes, ketchup, egg, ½ cup bouillon, salt, and pepper to the vegetable mixture. Mix very well, then mold mixture into a loaf and place in a 7" × 11" baking pan that has been coated with nonstick vegetable spray. Pour the remaining bouillon around the loaf; place on the middle rack of the oven and bake for 50 to 60 minutes, or until well browned.

NOTE: You might want to serve this with cranberry sauce on the side. You can also use ground veal, beef, or pork—or a combination!

turkey meat loaf florentine

4 to 6 servings

Meat loaf has been around for a long time, but lately we've discovered how versatile it can be. Here's a winner that's lower in fat. Why, it just gets better every time we make it.

2 pounds ground turkey	½ teaspoon bottled chopped garlic
1 box (10 ounces) frozen chopped spinach, thawed and well drained	4 cups (16 ounces) shredded mozzarella cheese
1 small onion, chopped	¼ teaspoon salt
½ teaspoon dried basil	¼ teaspoon pepper

Preheat the oven to 350°F. In a large bowl, mix together all the ingredients. Place the mixture in a 9" × 5" loaf pan that has been coated with nonstick vegetable spray or on a foil-lined cookie sheet (that has been coated with nonstick vegetable spray) and shape the mixture into a loaf. Bake for about 1 hour, or until cooked through.

lighter burgers

3 to 4 patties

*One of America's favorites is burgers. Well, here's a way
to enjoy our favorite—only lighter!*

1	pound ground turkey	¼	teaspoon salt
2	tablespoons chopped onion	¼	teaspoon pepper
2	tablespoons chopped fresh parsley	3	tablespoons dry bread crumbs
½	teaspoon dried oregano	3	tablespoons water
1	egg or egg white	3	tablespoons olive oil for frying (or as needed)
½	teaspoon garlic powder		

In a large bowl, combine all the ingredients, except the oil; mix well. Shape the mixture into 3 or 4 patties. In a large skillet, heat the oil over medium heat. Fry the burgers on each side until cooked through and no pink remains.

NOTE: These are also great broiled or grilled. You can serve them plain or topped with ranch dressing, spaghetti sauce, or even a "lite" cheese.

turkey "pot roast"

4 servings

*There sure won't be any arguments from the family when you
serve up this holiday-tasting dish on just any ol' day.*

4 turkey drumsticks	½ cup dry white wine
Vegetable oil for coating, plus 1 tablespoon for sautéing	1 tablespoon dried tarragon leaves
Salt to taste	1 can (28 ounces) tomatoes, drained and chopped
Pepper to taste	1 tablespoon cornstarch
1 cup chopped onion	2 tablespoons water
2 garlic cloves, minced	Chopped fresh parsley for garnish
12 ounces fresh mushrooms, sliced	

Preheat the oven to broil. Coat the drumsticks completely with oil, then sprinkle with salt and pepper. Place the drumsticks in a broiling pan and broil, turning until browned on all sides. Meanwhile, heat 1 tablespoon oil over medium-high heat in a Dutch oven or large skillet; add the onion and garlic and sauté until clear. Add the mushrooms and sauté for 5 to 6 minutes more, stirring occasionally. Add the wine, tarragon, and tomatoes, stirring to blend. Add the browned drumsticks, cover, and cook over medium-low heat for about 1 hour, or until the drumsticks are tender and done, stirring occasionally. Remove the drumsticks from the Dutch oven and place on a serving platter. In a small bowl, mix together the cornstarch and water. Raise heat to high, bring the Dutch oven contents to a boil, drizzle in the cornstarch mixture, and stir until thickened. Spoon over the drumsticks, sprinkle with chopped parsley, and serve.

taco turkey

2 to 3 servings

*Here's a new way to enjoy "light," with
lots of Southwest flavor.*

2½ to 3 pounds turkey
   drumsticks or thighs

1 package (1¼ ounces) taco
   seasoning mix
1 cup ketchup

Preheat the oven to 350°F. Place the turkey drumsticks in a shallow baking pan. In a small bowl, combine the taco seasoning mix and ketchup; pour over the drumsticks. Bake for 2 to 2½ hours, or until the turkey is done, basting occasionally. Serve immediately or refrigerate until ready to use.

NOTE: If you'd like to reheat these so they'll taste like an all-day Texas barbecue, warm them on the grill about 20 to 30 minutes before dinnertime. Turn drumsticks occasionally, basting.

cajun turkey

about 4 servings

*When we hear Cajun, we think spicy. Well, not true in this case—
here's Cajun at its most delicate. Hey!! You just found
another way to make turkey different and exciting!*

¼ cup all-purpose flour

1 egg, beaten

1 tablespoon milk

½ cup dry bread crumbs

4 tablespoons finely chopped
pecans

½ teaspoon pepper

About 1 pound boneless
fresh turkey breast slices

2 tablespoons vegetable oil

Place the flour in a shallow dish. In another shallow dish, combine the egg and milk. In a third shallow dish, combine the bread crumbs, pecans, and pepper. Dip each turkey breast slice in flour, in the egg mixture, then in the bread crumb mixture. Place the turkey slices on a large plate, cover with plastic wrap, and refrigerate for at least 1 hour to set the coating. When ready to cook, preheat the oven to 350°F. Heat the oil in a large nonstick skillet over medium-high heat until it sizzles, about 1 minute. Add the turkey slices and cook for 1½ to 2 minutes on each side, or until lightly browned. Remove from the skillet and place on a baking sheet that has been coated with nonstick vegetable spray; bake for 10 minutes or until done.

NOTE: Serve over hot cooked rice.

super bowl turkey strips
about 4 servings

The Super Bowl is such a big event—why, it's almost like a national holiday! And special times call for special food, so here's a treat that's fit for any special occasion. . . . It's an automatic party!

½ cup biscuit baking mix

½ cup cornflake crumbs or finely crushed cornflakes

½ teaspoon chili powder

½ teaspoon dried oregano

⅛ teaspoon pepper

2 eggs, slightly beaten

1 pound fresh turkey breast slices, cut into 1-inch strips

2 to 4 tablespoons butter or margarine, as needed

In a large bowl, combine the biscuit baking mix, cornflake crumbs, chili powder, oregano, and pepper. Place the beaten eggs in a shallow dish. Dip the turkey strips into the egg, then into the cornflake crumb mixture to coat. In a large skillet, heat the butter and sauté the coated strips over medium-low heat for 6 to 7 minutes, or until golden brown. Serve immediately or save for later use by placing the cooked strips on a cookie sheet, covering them, and storing in the refrigerator. Reheat in the oven or microwave when ready to serve.

NOTE: Serve on hot dog rolls with bottled chili sauce or salsa.

turkey "everything"

4 servings

Here's a way to make those turkey leftovers taste extra special.
They'll love it—even if they hate leftovers!

2 cups coarsely chopped cooked turkey	2 tablespoons lime juice
2 cups diced celery	1 teaspoon salt
½ cup cooked rice	¼ teaspoon black pepper
½ cup slivered almonds	¾ cup mayonnaise
⅓ cup chopped green bell pepper	½ cup mushroom soup, undiluted
2 tablespoons finely chopped onion	½ cup crushed potato chips

Preheat the oven to 350°F. In a large bowl, combine the turkey, celery, rice, almonds, green pepper, onion, lime juice, salt, and black pepper. In a medium-sized bowl, combine the mayonnaise and mushroom soup; add to the turkey mixture and stir to combine all the ingredients. Pour the mixture into a greased 1½-quart casserole dish. Top with crushed potato chips. Bake for 30 minutes.

NOTE: This is great for a main course, but you might also try serving it on toast points as an appetizer (call it "Turkey and Cream"), or even as an hors d'oeuvre spread.

turkey hash cakes

10 to 12 medium-sized pancakes

What a great way to use leftover turkey and potatoes with just a few other things you're bound to have on hand! Why, they'll probably beg you to make turkey just to get at these.

2 cups mashed potatoes

4 cups finely chopped cooked turkey

¼ cup chopped onions

¼ cup chopped green bell pepper

¼ cup dry bread crumbs

1 teaspoon salt

¾ teaspoon black pepper

¼ teaspoon garlic powder

¼ teaspoon paprika

¼ cup chopped fresh parsley

3 eggs, slightly beaten

¼ to ½ cup vegetable oil for frying, as needed

In a large bowl, combine all the ingredients except the egg and oil; mix well. Add the egg to the mixture, mix, then form into pancakes. Heat enough oil over medium-high heat to coat the bottom of a large skillet; fry the pancakes, adding additional oil as needed, until the pancakes are golden brown, then drain on paper towels. Serve hot.

NOTE: Leftover mashed potatoes will work well, but if you don't have any, instant mashed potatoes are fine, too. You can also use store-bought cooked boneless turkey parts—whatever's easiest!

buffalo-style turkey wings

1 to 2 servings

Next time you're left with just the turkey wings, don't worry!
Spice them up this way and they'll be the hit of the day!

2 cooked turkey wings

All-purpose flour for coating

Vegetable oil for frying

¼ cup (½ stick) butter or margarine, melted

¼ cup hot pepper sauce

Split the wings at each joint and discard tips. Place the flour in a shallow bowl; dip the wings in the flour. In a large skillet, heat the vegetable oil over medium-high heat; fry the wings for about 5 minutes, or until browned on both sides. Meanwhile, in a large bowl, combine the melted butter and hot pepper sauce. Remove the wings from the skillet and toss in the hot sauce mixture. Serve.

NOTE: If you want to serve these in true Buffalo style, serve with celery sticks and blue cheese dressing. This is a simple way to use leftover wings; if you want to make it for more than just 1 or 2 people, then cook up more wings in advance.

"one-pans"

chicken ratatouille

about 4 servings

A wonderful blend of fresh vegetables and chicken! In this you get great taste and vegetable abundance all rolled into one.

¼ cup vegetable oil

2 chicken breasts, skinned, boned, and cut into 1-inch pieces

1 medium-sized zucchini, thinly sliced

1 small eggplant, peeled and cut into 1-inch cubes

1 large onion, thinly sliced

1 medium-sized green bell pepper, seeded and cut into 1-inch pieces

½ pound mushrooms, sliced

1 can (14½ ounces) whole tomatoes, broken up

1 to 1½ teaspoons garlic powder

1½ teaspoons salt

1 teaspoon dried oregano

1 teaspoon dried basil, crushed

1 teaspoon parsley flakes

½ teaspoon black pepper

¼ cup chopped green olives

In a large skillet, heat the oil over medium heat. Add the chicken and sauté, stirring, for about 2 minutes. Add the zucchini, eggplant, onion, green pepper, and mushrooms. Cook, stirring occasionally, for about 15 minutes or until the vegetables are tender-crisp. Add the tomatoes, stirring gently. Stir in the remaining ingredients. Reduce heat and simmer, uncovered, for about 5 minutes. Place on a platter and serve.

NOTE: Serve over hot cooked rice or pasta.

tarragon chicken breast

4 to 6 servings

This chicken breast comes out tender, moist, and packed with flavor.
The tarragon gives it that French restaurant flair.

3 chicken breasts, split, skinned, and boned

Salt to taste

Pepper to taste

2 tablespoons butter or margarine

2 teaspoons dried tarragon, divided

¼ cup finely chopped onion

1 teaspoon finely minced garlic

½ cup dry white wine

1 cup chicken broth

Sprinkle the chicken with salt and pepper. In a large skillet, heat the butter over medium-high heat; add the chicken pieces and cook for about 3 minutes, or until golden brown. Turn the chicken pieces and add 1 teaspoon of tarragon. Continue cooking for about 6 minutes more, turning occasionally to keep the chicken from sticking. Remove the chicken and place on a warm platter. Add the onion, garlic, and wine to the skillet. Cook for about 3 minutes more, stirring occasionally. Add the broth and bring to a boil; boil for 3 minutes. Add the remaining 1 teaspoon tarragon and return the chicken to the skillet. Cook for about 5 minutes more, or until the chicken is fork-tender and done and the sauce has thickened slightly, turning the chicken to coat it with the sauce.

NOTE: Serve over hot cooked rice.

chicken and sausage

about 4 servings

*In the mood for a quick skillet dinner that tastes like
it cooked all day? Here it is!*

1 tablespoon olive or vegetable oil	1 medium-sized green bell pepper, cut into 2-inch strips
2 skinless and boneless chicken breasts, cut into strips	2 garlic cloves, minced
½ pound Italian sausage, casing removed, crumbled	1 can (11⅛ ounces) Italian-style tomato soup
	1 cup water

In a large skillet, heat the oil over medium-high heat. Add the chicken and cook until browned. Remove the chicken; set aside. Reduce the heat to medium. In the same skillet, cook the sausage, green pepper, and garlic, stirring, until the sausage is browned and the pepper is tender. Spoon off the fat. Stir in the soup and water. Heat to boiling and return the chicken to the skillet. Reduce the heat to low. Cover; cook for 6 to 7 minutes more, or until the chicken is no longer pink, stirring occasionally.

NOTE: Serve over hot cooked rice.

curry chicken

3 to 4 servings

If you don't try this wonderful combination of Middle Eastern flavors,
you'll really be missing out. This one is bound to please you,
your family . . . in fact, anyone who's lucky enough
to be invited to your table.

4 tablespoons vegetable oil, divided
2 onions, finely chopped
1 chicken (2½ to 3 pounds), cut into 8 pieces
1 tablespoon curry powder
½ cup white wine
¼ teaspoon garlic powder
¼ teaspoon thyme leaves

¼ teaspoon ground nutmeg
1 can (14½ ounces) whole tomatoes, drained
1 apple, peeled, cored, and cut into cubes
3 tablespoons heavy cream
¼ cup raisins
½ teaspoon lemon juice

In a large skillet, heat 2 tablespoons oil over medium-high heat; add the onions and sauté until transparent. Remove the onions from the skillet; set aside. Heat remaining 2 tablespoons oil in the skillet, add the chicken, brown on all sides, and return the onions to the skillet. Add the curry powder, wine, garlic powder, thyme, nutmeg, and tomatoes; mix well. Reduce the heat and simmer, covered, for about 20 minutes. Add the apple, heavy cream, and raisins; cook for 6 to 8 minutes more, or until chicken is fork-tender and no pink remains. Add the lemon juice, stir, and serve.

108

chicken with summer vegetables

3 to 4 servings

*Crunchy, fresh-tasting, and summery all add up to Chicken
with Summer Vegetables. And with the price and
popularity of both, it's bonus time.*

1 tablespoon butter or
  margarine

2 chicken breasts, split,
  skinned, and boned

1 medium-sized onion, cut into
  wedges

1 garlic clove, minced

1 medium-sized tomato, cut
  into wedges

1 medium-sized zucchini, cut
  into strips

1 medium-sized yellow
  squash, cut into strips

¼ teaspoon salt

¼ teaspoon pepper

½ teaspoon dried basil

In a large skillet, melt the butter over medium heat; add the
chicken and cook for 6 to 8 minutes, or until browned on both
sides. Add the remaining ingredients. Reduce the heat to low and
simmer, covered, for 5 to 7 minutes more, or until the chicken is
fork-tender and no pink remains and the vegetables are tender-
crisp.

109

main courses

italian chicken and rice

3 to 4 servings

*When you want to combine yesterday's flavors with today's
"easy," try this one. It'll taste like you spent hours at
the stove like Mama did, but not with
this one. . . . Uh! Uh!*

1¼	cups water	⅓	cup finely chopped onion
1	cup uncooked rice	¼	teaspoon garlic powder
1	can (14½ ounces) whole tomatoes, undrained and broken up	2	teaspoons Italian seasoning, divided
½	pound processed cheese spread (like Velveeta®), cubed	1	chicken (2½ to 3 pounds), cut into 8 pieces
		⅔	cup grated Parmesan cheese

Preheat the oven to 375°F. In a greased 9" × 13" baking pan, mix the water, rice, tomatoes, cheese spread, onion, garlic powder, and 1 teaspoon Italian seasoning. Top the mixture with the chicken pieces and sprinkle with Parmesan cheese and remaining Italian seasoning. Bake for 50 to 60 minutes, or until the chicken is fork-tender and no pink remains. Remove from the oven and let stand for 5 to 10 minutes before serving.

skillet chicken

3 to 4 servings

Homemade-tasting, fast, and easy—yup! That's just what we need with today's busy schedules.

1 envelope (from a 2-ounce box) onion or onion-mushroom soup mix

¼ cup olive or vegetable oil

¼ cup water

1 tablespoon lime or lemon juice

½ teaspoon garlic powder

2 chicken breasts, skinned, boned, and cut into thin strips

1 package (10 ounces) frozen mixed vegetables, partially thawed and drained

½ cup spaghetti sauce

¼ cup red wine

In a large skillet, blend together the soup mix, oil, water, lime juice, and garlic powder; let stand for 5 minutes. Bring to a boil, then stir in the chicken, vegetables, spaghetti sauce, and wine. Cook, uncovered, for 5 to 10 minutes, stirring frequently, until the chicken is fork-tender and no pink remains.

NOTE: Serve over hot cooked rice.

chicken with zucchini and tomatoes

3 to 4 servings

Bring a little bit of summer to your table
(at any time of year!).

2 tablespoons olive oil

2 chicken breasts, split and skinned

2 small zucchini, cut into ¼-inch slices

1 can (14½ ounces) stewed tomatoes

½ teaspoon Italian seasoning

¼ teaspoon salt

¼ teaspoon pepper

¼ teaspoon garlic powder

In a large skillet, heat the oil over medium-high heat. Add the chicken and cook until browned on both sides, about 10 minutes. Drain off excess fat. Add the remaining ingredients. Reduce the heat to medium-low, cover, and cook for 20 to 30 minutes, or until the chicken is fork-tender and no pink remains, stirring occasionally.

french chicken breasts in wine sauce

3 to 4 servings

*Fancy French again, huh? Well, if you're talking about taste,
yes, indeed! But if you're talking about a lot of work—
uh! uh! See how easy!*

2 tablespoons butter or
margarine

2 chicken breasts, split,
skinned, and boned

1 can or jar (about 4 ounces)
sliced mushrooms, drained

¼ cup dry white wine

½ teaspoon thyme leaves

½ teaspoon dried tarragon

½ teaspoon parsley flakes

In a large skillet, melt the butter over medium heat; add the
chicken and cook for 6 to 8 minutes per side, or until browned on
both sides. Add the remaining ingredients. Cover, reduce heat to
low, and cook for 5 to 10 minutes, or until the chicken is fork-
tender and no pink remains.

sausage and chicken livers

4 servings

*If hearty, stick-to-the-ribs food is what you want, you've got all
that goodness right here. (Have you checked the price of
chicken livers in the markets?? Wow!!
Great deal for a great meal.)*

½ pound hot Italian sausage,
casing removed, broken up

2 bunches scallions, chopped

¼ pound mushrooms, chopped

2 celery stalks, chopped

1 pound chicken livers

1 tablespoon soy sauce

2 tablespoons minced fresh
parsley

Place the sausage meat in a large skillet and sauté over medium-high heat until lightly browned. Add the scallions, mushrooms, and celery; sauté lightly. Add the chicken livers. Cook over
high heat for 5 to 10 minutes, stirring occasionally. Stir in the soy
sauce. Reduce the heat and simmer for 5 minutes more, stirring
occasionally. Garnish with parsley.

NOTE: Serve over hot cooked rice.

company stew

3 to 4 servings

*It's that little bit different 'cause it's summery light,
quick, and smart. Wow, you're a whiz!*

4 tablespoons vegetable oil

2 pounds dark meat turkey,
cut into 1-inch chunks

2 garlic cloves, crushed

1 large onion, chopped

1 envelope onion soup mix
(from a 2-ounce box)

1 can (15 ounces) tomato
sauce

2 cups water

½ cup dry red wine

1 tablespoon Worcestershire
sauce

1 bay leaf

In a large saucepan, heat the oil over medium heat; add the
turkey chunks and brown lightly. Add the garlic and onion and
cook for 4 to 5 minutes more. Stir in the remaining ingredients;
bring to a boil. Reduce the heat and simmer for 45 minutes, stirring
occasionally. **Remove the bay leaf before serving.**

NOTE: Serve over hot cooked rice or noodles.

black-eyed pea skillet

about 4 servings

Here's a fast "one-pot" that's good for the family and filled with the homemade flavors that everybody'll remember with love.

2 tablespoons vegetable oil	1 can (14½ ounces) whole tomatoes, undrained and coarsely chopped
1 pound ground turkey	
1½ cups chopped onion	½ teaspoon salt
1 cup chopped green bell pepper	¼ teaspoon black pepper
2 cans (16 ounces each) black-eyed peas, drained	

In a large skillet, heat the oil over medium heat; add the ground turkey, onion, and green bell pepper and cook until the turkey is browned, stirring to crumble the meat. Drain off the liquid. Add the remaining ingredients; bring to a boil, reduce heat, and simmer for 30 minutes, stirring often.

NOTE: Go ahead and add your own seasoning favorites. Anything from basil to oregano, chili powder, hot pepper sauce, or Cajun seasoning will work!

two-bean turkey chili

6 servings
(about 6 cups chili)

Most chili dishes need hours of cooking to blend their flavors.
If we don't have that kind of time, we can add some extra
taste right at the beginning, and have chili in minutes.

1 to 2 tablespoons vegetable oil

1 pound Italian turkey sausage, casing removed

1 large onion, chopped (about 1½ cups)

1 can (15½ ounces) black beans, undrained

1 can (15½ ounces) kidney or pinto beans, undrained

1 cup beef broth

1 can (7 to 8 ounces) whole kernel corn, drained

¾ cup picante sauce

1 green bell pepper, cut into ¾-inch pieces

1 red bell pepper, cut into ¾-inch pieces

In a large saucepan or Dutch oven, heat the oil over medium-high heat. Break up the sausage and sauté with the onion until the sausage is browned and the onion is tender; drain. Add the remaining ingredients and bring to a boil. Reduce the heat and simmer, uncovered, for about 15 minutes, stirring occasionally, or until the chili reaches desired consistency. Serve.

NOTE: Top with sour cream, shredded cheese, and/or chopped cilantro, and serve with additional picante sauce.

chuck wagon mix

about 4 servings

*Here's a whole mess o' that great barbecue flavor we love . . .
and in just one pan.*

1 tablespoon vegetable oil

1 pound smoked turkey kielbasa, cut into ½-inch slices

3 cups cooked rice

1 can (about 16 ounces) red kidney or pinto beans, rinsed and drained

½ cup bottled hickory-smoked barbecue sauce

In a large skillet, heat the oil over medium-high heat; brown the kielbasa, drain excess fat, then return the kielbasa to the skillet. Stir in the rice, beans, and sauce. Cook over medium-high heat until thoroughly heated, about 5 minutes, stirring occasionally.

taste adventures

honey chicken

3 to 4 servings

*You can taste the Southern hospitality in this one. It's
bound to become one of your family's favorites.*

¼ pound (½ cup) butter

1 cup all-purpose flour

2 teaspoons salt

¼ teaspoon pepper

2 teaspoons paprika

1 chicken (2½ to 3 pounds),
cut into 8 pieces

SAUCE

¼ cup melted butter

½ cup honey

¼ cup lemon juice

Preheat the oven to 400°F. Melt the ¼ pound of butter in a
9" × 13" baking pan in the oven; remove the baking pan from the
oven. In a shallow bowl, mix together the flour, salt, pepper, and
paprika; dip the chicken pieces into the flour mixture. Add the
chicken pieces to the pan, coat completely with butter, then bake
for 30 minutes, skin side down, in a single layer. Meanwhile, in a
small bowl, mix together the sauce ingredients. Turn the chicken,
then cover with sauce. Bake for 30 minutes more, or until the
chicken is fork-tender and no pink remains. Spoon the sauce over
the chicken again and serve.

roast chicken and kiwi with raspberry glaze

3 to 4 servings

Want something a little fancy-looking for company? Well, here's
a way to make roast chicken look like a million dollars,
but it's not harder or more expensive to make. . . .
Like I said, just a little fancy-looking.

1 chicken (about 3 pounds), cut in half

¼ to ½ teaspoon salt

⅛ teaspoon pepper

2 tablespoons butter or margarine, melted

RASPBERRY GLAZE

½ cup seedless raspberry preserves

¼ cup red or sweet wine

Grated peel of ½ lemon

2 kiwifruit, peeled and cut into 4 to 5 slices per kiwi

Preheat the oven to 400°F. Sprinkle the chicken with salt and pepper. Place the chicken, skin side up, in a single layer in a 9" × 13" baking pan. Brush the chicken with melted butter. Bake for about 45 minutes, basting frequently, or until the chicken is fork-tender and no pink remains. Drain off the fat. Meanwhile, in a medium-sized saucepan, mix together all the Raspberry Glaze ingredients. Cook over a low heat for about 5 minutes or until slightly thickened. Spoon the glaze over the chicken, then baste generously. Top with the kiwi slices, dividing the slices evenly over both halves of the chicken. Return to the oven and bake for about 3 minutes more, or until the fruit and chicken are well glazed.

thai chicken

4 to 6 servings

With chicken and Asian flavors being so popular, it makes sense to put them together. This is one of the most requested recipes from my TV show. You'll see why. . . .

2	cups picante sauce	1	teaspoon ground ginger
½	cup chunky peanut butter	12	ounces cooked fettuccine
¼	cup honey	2	tablespoons vegetable oil
¼	cup orange juice	3	chicken breasts, split,
2	teaspoons soy sauce		skinned, and boned

In a small saucepan, combine the picante sauce, peanut butter, honey, orange juice, soy sauce, and ginger; cook over low heat, stirring, until blended and smooth. Reserve ¼ cup picante sauce mixture; toss the remaining picante sauce mixture with hot cooked fettuccine and place on serving platter. In a large skillet, heat the oil over medium-high heat; place the chicken in the skillet and cook for 5 to 10 minutes, or until browned and done. Place the chicken over the fettuccine, spoon the reserved picante sauce mixture over the chicken, and serve.

123

chicken egg foo-yung

two 10-inch pancakes

This is that simple Chinese dish that's simply delicious—and now you don't have to go to a Chinese restaurant to enjoy it.

6   eggs, well beaten

1   teaspoon salt

½   teaspoon sesame oil

5   tablespoons vegetable oil, divided

2   scallions, finely chopped

2   celery stalks, finely chopped

1   carrot, finely chopped

½   cup drained canned bean sprouts (one 14½-ounce can contains about 1½ cups drained bean sprouts)

2   teaspoons sugar

½   of a cooked boneless and skinless chicken breast, shredded

In a large bowl, combine the egg, salt, and sesame oil. In a large (10-inch) nonstick skillet, heat 1 tablespoon of the vegetable oil over medium-high heat; sauté the scallions, celery, and carrot for about 1 minute. Stir in the bean sprouts and sugar. Remove from the skillet and add the vegetable mixture to the egg mixture. Add the shredded chicken and mix together. In the same skillet, heat 2 tablespoons vegetable oil over medium-high heat; place 1¼ cups of the chicken mixture into the hot skillet. Cook for 2 minutes over medium-high heat, reduce the heat to low, cover, and cook for 3 minutes more. Flip the pancake and cook, uncovered, for 2½ minutes more. Place on a serving plate. Repeat the process with the remaining chicken mixture for the second pancake.

NOTE: If you don't have sesame oil, you can substitute vegetable oil.

chicken fried rice

3 to 4 servings
(about 6 cups)

*Here's another Chinese restaurant favorite that
you can whip up in your own kitchen.*

¼ cup vegetable oil

2½ cups chunked boneless
and skinless chicken breast
(about 1¼ pounds)

2 eggs, lightly beaten

1 can or jar (about 4 ounces)
mushrooms, drained

½ to 1 teaspoon salt

Freshly ground black pepper to
taste

4 cups cooked rice

2 tablespoons soy sauce

½ cup chopped scallion

In a large skillet or wok, heat the oil over high heat; add the chicken and stir-fry for about 3 minutes, or until cooked and no pink remains, stirring constantly. Add the eggs, mushrooms, salt, and pepper, and stir-fry over medium heat for 3 to 4 minutes, stirring constantly. Add the rice and soy sauce and cook for 3 to 4 minutes more, stirring frequently. Add the chopped scallion, remove from the skillet, and serve.

NOTE: This can be a whole meal or a side dish! Try it with imitation crabmeat, beef, shrimp, or pork—whatever you'd like! Just adjust the first stir-frying time accordingly so that any of these items is completely cooked before adding the additional ingredients. Or— you may just want to start with already-cooked or leftover chicken. Then you'd only have to start by stir-frying it alone for about 1 minute, just enough to warm it.

main courses

nutty drummers

4 servings

Satisfy everybody with this great combination of Asian flavorings and that most fun chicken part . . . drumsticks!

3 tablespoons vegetable oil	2 tablespoons chunky-style peanut butter
8 chicken drumsticks	
¾ cup chicken broth	2 scallions, sliced
1 tablespoon lemon juice	¼ teaspoon salt
1 tablespoon Worcestershire sauce	¼ teaspoon garlic powder
	¼ teaspoon ground ginger
1 tablespoon honey	¼ cup chopped peanuts

Preheat the oven to 375°F. In a large skillet, heat the oil over medium-high heat. Add the drumsticks and cook, turning frequently, for about 10 minutes, or until lightly browned on all sides. Place the drumsticks in a 7" × 11" baking dish and drain the oil from the skillet. Place the remaining ingredients, except the peanuts, in the skillet; stir to mix well. Cook over medium heat, stirring constantly, for about 3 minutes, or until slightly thickened. Pour the sauce over the drumsticks. Bake, covered, for about 30 to 35 minutes, or until the chicken is fork-tender and no pink remains. Place the drumsticks on a serving platter and cover with the sauce. Sprinkle with peanuts.

chicken breasts with balsamic vinegar

6 to 8 servings

The balsamic vinegar (which is now in all of our supermarkets) really gives the chicken a fine, elegant taste. The right amount of sparkle, the right amount of mild sweetness, and the right amount of raves, too.

4 tablespoons all-purpose flour	¾ pound mushrooms, cleaned and cut in half
¼ teaspoon salt	¾ cup chicken broth
¼ teaspoon pepper	¼ cup balsamic vinegar
4 chicken breasts, split, skinned, and boned	2 bay leaves
2 tablespoons olive oil	¼ teaspoon thyme leaves
6 peeled garlic cloves	1 tablespoon butter or margarine (optional)

Place the flour in a shallow dish and season with salt and pepper; dredge the chicken in the flour mixture. In a large skillet, heat the oil over medium heat; add the chicken and cook until browned on one side, about 3 minutes. Turn the chicken, then add the garlic and mushrooms. Continue cooking for 3 minutes more, moving the garlic and mushrooms around in the skillet. Add the chicken broth, vinegar, bay leaves, and thyme. Cover tightly, reduce the heat to medium-low, and cook for 10 minutes, turning the chicken occasionally. Transfer the chicken to a serving platter and keep warm. Raise the heat to medium, and cook the pan juices, uncovered, for 7 minutes more. Add butter, if desired; **remove and discard the bay leaves,** stir mixture, then spoon over chicken.

NOTE: If your skillet isn't large enough to cook all of the chicken together, use two smaller skillets and split the ingredients between them.

chicken avocado melt

3 to 4 servings

*Sounds so "in," doesn't it? Well, it is! It's in my recipe box
because it's filled with good flavor but not a lot of work.
Yes, avocados are getting more and more popular
every day. And they aren't as expensive as
they used to be, either—that
makes them better, too.*

2 tablespoons cornstarch

1 teaspoon ground cumin

1 teaspoon garlic salt

1 egg, slightly beaten

1 tablespoon water

⅓ cup cornmeal

2 chicken breasts, split, skinned, boned, and flattened

3 tablespoons vegetable oil

1 firm, ripe avocado, peeled and cut into 8 slices

1½ cups (6 ounces) shredded Monterey Jack or Cheddar cheese

½ cup sour cream, divided

¼ cup sliced scallion tops

¼ cup chopped red bell pepper

Preheat the oven to 350°F. In a shallow dish, mix together the cornstarch, cumin, and garlic salt; set aside. In a small bowl, mix the egg and water; place the cornmeal in another small bowl. Dredge the chicken, one piece at a time, in the cornstarch mixture, then dip in the egg mixture, then the cornmeal, turning to coat evenly. Heat the oil over a medium temperature in a large skillet; add the chicken, cooking for 2 minutes on each side. Remove the chicken to a shallow baking pan; place the avocado slices over the chicken and top with shredded cheese. Bake for about 15 minutes, or until the chicken is fork-tender and the cheese has melted. Remove from the oven and top with sour cream, sliced scallion, and red pepper, dividing them evenly over the chicken pieces.

north african chicken

3 to 4 servings

An exotic and fun way to serve chicken, this is great for that dinner party where the taste becomes the conversation piece. (And it's perfect 'cause it can be made ahead and reheated just before serving.)

1 chicken (2½ to 3 pounds), cut into 8 pieces

MOROCCAN SAUCE
½ cup chicken broth
1 can (14½ ounces) stewed tomatoes, coarsely chopped
1 potato, cubed

1 carrot, sliced
1 onion, chopped
6 garlic cloves, minced
1½ teaspoons turmeric
½ teaspoon ground cumin (or to taste)
¼ cup packed raisins
⅛ teaspoon cayenne pepper

Preheat the oven to 350°F. Place the chicken in a 9" × 13" baking pan and bake for 30 minutes, basting with the pan juices. Meanwhile, in a Dutch oven, combine all the sauce ingredients and cook for 20 minutes over medium heat, stirring occasionally. Place the partially cooked chicken in the sauce, cover, reduce the heat to low, and simmer for 30 minutes, or until the chicken is fork-tender and no pink remains.

NOTE: Serve over hot cooked orzo pasta or pastina.

129

provolone chicken

3 to 4 servings

*Another fine example of how fancy-tasting and fancy-looking
can still be easy-cooking. This proves
that simple is sometimes best.*

½ cup seasoned bread crumbs

2 chicken breasts, split, skinned, boned, and flattened

½ teaspoon dried oregano

4 slices provolone cheese

Sprig of fresh parsley, chopped

1 teaspoon butter or margarine (optional)

Preheat the oven to 425°F. Place the bread crumbs in a shallow dish; press both sides of the chicken into the crumbs. Place the coated chicken pieces in a greased 9" × 13" baking pan. Sprinkle with oregano, top with provolone cheese, sprinkle with parsley, and dot with butter. Bake for 15 to 20 minutes, or until done, then remove from the baking pan and serve.

roast chicken with curried honey mustard sauce

3 to 4 servings

Here's a nice combination of flavors that smacks of faraway exotic places, but it's as comfortable as your own kitchen. And get a load of how easy it is!

SAUCE
2 chicken breasts, split

1 small onion, chopped
⅓ cup honey
⅓ cup spicy mustard
1 tablespoon curry powder
2 garlic cloves, minced

Preheat the oven to 350°F. In a small bowl, mix together the sauce ingredients. Place the chicken, skin side up, in a single layer in a large baking pan. Pour the sauce over the chicken and bake for about 1 hour, or until the chicken is fork-tender and no pink remains, basting every 15 minutes.

NOTE: I like this served over hot cooked rice.

chicken with apple salsa

4 servings

*Make tonight's chicken seem new and exciting with this
contest winner full of Pennsylvania Dutch touches.*

8 chicken thighs, boned and
skinned

½ fresh lemon or lime

½ teaspoon pepper

1 tablespoon dark brown
sugar

1 cup bottled chili sauce

1 cup peeled, cored, and
chopped Granny Smith apple
(about 1 medium-sized
apple)

Crushed corn chips for garnish

Place the chicken thighs on a broiler pan. Squeeze the juice
from the ½ lemon evenly over the chicken, then sprinkle with pepper. Broil about 6 inches from the heat for about 8 to 10 minutes,
or until the chicken is fork-tender and no pink remains, turning
once; set aside. In a nonstick saucepan, combine the dark brown
sugar and chili sauce. Place over medium heat, add the chopped
apple, and cook for 10 minutes, stirring occasionally. Spread the
apple mixture evenly over the chicken, then return it to the broiler
for 2 minutes more. Garnish with crushed corn chips.

NOTE: Any tart apple will work here.

ranch chicken breasts

3 to 4 servings

Since we're always looking for different things to do with chicken,
here's a special way that'll look and taste like it's lots
of work and money, but it's really "easy as
a lark" (and inexpensive, too)!

2½ cups pineapple juice

2 packages (1 ounce each) milk recipe ranch salad dressing mix

2 chicken breasts, split and boned

1 tablespoon cornstarch

1 tablespoon water

Chopped fresh parsley for garnish

In a small saucepan, whisk together the pineapple juice and dressing mix. Place the chicken breasts in a 9-inch square baking pan and pour half the juice mixture over breasts; reserve the remaining juice mixture. Cover and marinate, turning occasionally, for at least 2 hours in refrigerator (overnight is OK, too). Preheat the oven to 350°F. Bake the marinated breasts for about 45 minutes, or until no pink remains. Meanwhile, in a small saucepan, combine the cornstarch, water, and remaining juice mixture. Heat to thicken the mixture, then brush the cooked breasts with the sauce. Serve garnished with chopped parsley.

peppered raspberry chicken

4 servings

Very trendy, difficult, and gourmet-sounding, right? Well, it's not!
Go ahead and enjoy this great combination of flavors.
It's as easy as pie.... No ... easier than pie.

4 whole chicken legs (thigh and drumstick attached)	½ cup seedless red raspberry jam
½ teaspoon salt	2 tablespoons balsamic vinegar
¼ teaspoon black pepper	
2 tablespoons butter or margarine, melted	1 tablespoon soy sauce
	¼ teaspoon crushed red pepper
	Fresh parsley sprigs for garnish

Preheat the oven to 375°F. Place the chicken in a large broiler-proof baking pan. Sprinkle with salt and black pepper; drizzle butter over the chicken. Bake, basting occasionally, for 45 to 50 minutes, or until the chicken is golden. Meanwhile, in a small saucepan, mix together the jam, vinegar, soy sauce, and red pepper. Cook over medium heat until smooth, stirring occasionally. Spoon the sauce over the chicken; bake for 5 minutes more, or until the chicken is glazed and fork-tender. Heat the oven to broil, baste the chicken, and broil for 4 to 5 minutes or until the chicken is golden brown. Arrange the chicken on a platter and garnish with parsley.

family favorites

MAMA'S CHICKEN SOUP   137

FRIDAY NIGHT ROASTED CHICKEN   138

MARSALA CHICKEN   139

NEW CHICKEN CACCIATORE   140

EASY BARBECUED CHICKEN   141

OVEN-FRIED CHICKEN   142

HOMESTYLE CHICKEN   143

EASY CHICKEN FRICASSEE   144

FANCY FAST CHICKEN   145

MAMA'S OLD-FASHIONED STUFFING   146

MASHED POTATO STUFFING   147

VEGETABLE HARVEST STUFFING   148

mama's chicken soup

8 to 10 servings

One of my most requested recipes is Chicken Soup. Here's the way my Mama made it, but with a few different touches, you can make it your very own.

1 chicken (3 to 4 pounds), cut into 8 pieces

4 quarts cold water

3 to 4 carrots, peeled and cut into chunks

2 to 3 celery stalks, cut into chunks

2 medium-sized onions, cut into chunks

Salt to taste

Pepper to taste

Rinse the chicken under cold running water. Place all the ingredients in a soup pot and bring to a boil. Reduce the heat, cover, and simmer for 2 to 3 hours, or until chicken meat falls off the bones, stirring occasionally.

NOTE: You can adjust the cooking time according to how much chicken flavor you want the soup to have—I like to wait until the meat falls off the bones. Here are some variations I like: Strain the soup for a clear broth or serve it with just the veggies in it (reserving the chicken to make a great salad); use white pepper instead of black so there are no specks; use different amounts of any of the vegetables; add fresh dill or parsley, a couple of parsnips, or garlic cloves or all of those.

friday night roasted chicken

3 to 4 servings

Basic homestyle chicken, so there are lots
of good memories here.

1 teaspoon paprika	4 teaspoons vegetable oil
1 teaspoon onion powder	½ teaspoon pepper
1 teaspoon garlic powder	½ teaspoon seasoned salt
1 teaspoon salt	1 whole chicken (about 3 pounds)

In a small bowl, mix together all the ingredients except the chicken. Place the chicken in a roasting pan and rub the seasoning mixture into the chicken until well coated. Bake, uncovered, for 1½ hours, or until the chicken is done and the skin is crispy, using a pastry brush to baste occasionally.

138

marsala chicken

4 to 6 servings

*The only thing fancy about this dish is the
taste—and boy, is that fancy!*

½ cup all-purpose flour	½ cup marsala wine or sherry
1¼ teaspoons salt, divided	1 cup chicken bouillon
3 chicken breasts, split, skinned, and boned	½ teaspoon pepper
	½ teaspoon garlic powder
¼ cup vegetable oil	1 tablespoon parsley flakes
¼ cup (½ stick) margarine	1 cup sliced mushrooms

In a shallow dish, mix together the flour and 1 teaspoon salt; dredge the chicken in the flour mixture. In a large skillet, heat the oil over medium-high heat; sauté the chicken for 6 to 8 minutes, or until browned on both sides. Remove the chicken from the skillet and set aside; add the margarine, wine, bouillon, ¼ teaspoon salt, pepper, garlic powder, and parsley. Reduce the heat and simmer for 2 to 3 minutes. Return the chicken to the skillet; add the mushrooms, cover, and simmer for 10 minutes more, or until the chicken is fork-tender and no pink remains.

family favorites

new chicken cacciatore

about 3 servings

*Here's an old favorite, but with a little "today" mixed in.
Plus, with a few different flavorings . . . boy,
will your taste buds be impressed!*

¼ cup all-purpose flour

1 teaspoon salt

½ teaspoon black pepper

1 pound chicken breasts, skinned

1 pound chicken thighs, skinned

2 tablespoons olive oil

¾ cup picante sauce

1 can (8 ounces) tomato sauce

¼ cup dry red wine

8 ounces (½ pound) mushrooms, sliced

2 garlic cloves, minced

1 teaspoon dried basil

1 teaspoon dried oregano

1 green bell pepper, cut into short, thin strips

In a large shallow pan, combine the flour, salt, and pepper. Coat the chicken in the flour mixture. Heat the oil in a large, deep skillet or Dutch oven. Cook the chicken for about 8 minutes, or until lightly browned on both sides; drain. Add the remaining ingredients, except the green pepper strips; cover and simmer for 20 minutes. Stir in the pepper strips and simmer, uncovered, for about 10 minutes more, or until the chicken is fork-tender, no pink remains, and the liquid has thickened. Serve with the sauce from the pan.

NOTE: You can use chicken breasts and thighs, as indicated above, or 2 pounds of either part by itself.

family favorites

easy barbecued chicken

about 4 servings

Here's the simplest tip on how to enjoy the great barbecue flavor that we all love. Believe it or not, this is the way so many of the BBQ restaurants do it.

1 chicken (2½ to 3 pounds), cut into eight pieces

1 bottle (18 ounces) barbecue sauce (1½ cups)

Preheat the oven to 350°F. Place the chicken in a broiler-proof roasting pan and bake for 30 minutes; pour off liquid. Pour the barbecue sauce over the chicken, distributing it evenly, then bake for another 20 to 30 minutes, or until the chicken is fork-tender and no pink remains, basting occasionally. Turn the oven to broil and leave the chicken under the broiler for 3 to 5 minutes to brown slightly. Serve immediately.

NOTE: This is great for a summer barbecue, too: instead of putting the chicken under the broiler for 3 to 5 minutes after baking, place it on the grill for a few minutes, until browned. By the way, the secret to keeping the sauce on the chicken is draining off the excess liquid before adding the barbecue sauce.

oven-fried chicken

3 to 4 servings

Everybody loves the taste of fried chicken, but nobody wants the mess of making it. Here's a smarter way to get all that great taste!

¼ cup (½ stick) margarine

⅓ cup all-purpose flour

1 teaspoon salt

¼ teaspoon pepper

¼ teaspoon dried thyme

1 teaspoon paprika

1 chicken (about 3 pounds), cut into 8 pieces

Preheat the oven to 425°F. Place the margarine in a 9" × 13" baking pan and place it in the oven until the margarine melts. Meanwhile, in a shallow dish, combine the remaining ingredients, except the chicken. Coat the chicken with the flour mixture, then dip it in the melted margarine to lightly coat. Place the chicken, skin side down, on a baking rack and place the rack in a baking pan. (This will allow the fat to drip off chicken.) Bake for 30 minutes, turn, bake for 15 minutes more, or until the chicken is fork-tender and no pink remains.

homestyle chicken

3 to 4 servings

*This is a one-pan version of our family's favorite
roast chicken dinner.*

1 tablespoon dried basil

2 teaspoons paprika

¾ teaspoon salt

½ teaspoon onion powder

¼ teaspoon garlic powder

½ teaspoon thyme leaves

⅛ teaspoon cayenne pepper

¼ teaspoon ground nutmeg

¼ teaspoon chili powder

¼ teaspoon ground coriander (optional)

2 tablespoons vegetable oil

2 tablespoons water

1 can (8 ounces) tomato sauce

1 tablespoon lemon juice

1 chicken (2½ to 3 pounds), cut into 8 pieces

1½ pounds potatoes, peeled and cut into small cubes

Preheat the oven to 425°F. In a medium-sized bowl, mix together the basil, paprika, salt, onion and garlic powders, thyme, cayenne pepper, nutmeg, chili powder, and coriander; stir in the oil, water, tomato sauce, and lemon juice. Place the chicken pieces in a 9" × 13" baking pan that has been coated with nonstick vegetable spray. Arrange the potatoes around the chicken. Pour the seasoning mixture over the chicken and potatoes, generously coating them. Cover with aluminum foil and bake for 50 minutes, basting occasionally; uncover and bake for 10 minutes more, or until the potatoes are tender and the chicken is fork-tender, with no pink remaining.

NOTE: If you prefer to use chicken breasts, here's how: Cover and bake just the potatoes in the seasoning mixture for 30 minutes; add 2 split, skinned, and boned chicken breasts and coat with the pan ingredients; cover the pan and continue baking for 20 minutes more, until the chicken is fork-tender and no pink remains.

143

family favorites

easy chicken fricassee

about 8 servings

The flavor and aroma of the good old days—
but this way it's "today easy."

4 pounds chicken wings

4 tablespoons vegetable oil

2 large onions, chopped

4 packets (¾ ounce each) mushrooms in brown gravy mix, made according to package directions (each packet should make 1 cup)

1 teaspoon paprika

1 teaspoon sugar

½ teaspoon garlic powder

½ teaspoon salt

½ teaspoon pepper

MEATBALLS

3 pounds ground beef

2 eggs

1 cup bread crumbs

1 teaspoon onion powder

Dash salt

Dash pepper

Split the wings at each joint and discard the tips; rinse, then pat dry and set aside. In a large pot, heat the oil over medium-high heat; add the onions and sauté until soft. Add the wings to the pot and cook until golden, about 10 minutes, stirring occasionally. Add the prepared gravy, paprika, sugar, garlic powder, ½ teaspoon salt, and ½ teaspoon pepper and cook over medium heat for about 20 minutes. Meanwhile, in a large bowl, mix together the meatball ingredients; roll into small meatballs. Gradually add the meatballs to the pot and cook for 20 to 30 minutes more, or until the meatballs are done, stirring frequently and carefully (so as not to break up the meatballs).

NOTE: Adjust the seasonings to your taste and serve over your favorite shape egg noodles. This tastes even better the second day, so if you have time, try making it a day before you plan to serve it.

fancy fast chicken

4 to 6 servings

*Want to impress your company? Here's a way to do it without
a lot of extra work. Now, that's impressive! (This is still
my most requested chicken recipe. . . . Thanks, Rick!)*

3 whole chicken breasts, split and skinned

6 slices Swiss cheese (1 ounce each)

¼ pound fresh mushrooms, sliced (optional)

1 can (10¾ ounces) condensed cream of chicken soup

½ cup dry white wine

2 cups herb-seasoned stuffing mix

8 tablespoons (1 stick) butter or margarine, melted

Preheat the oven to 350°F. Place the chicken in a lightly greased 9" × 13" baking pan. Top each chicken piece with a slice of Swiss cheese. Arrange the sliced mushrooms over the cheese, if desired. In a small bowl, mix together the soup and wine; pour over the chicken. Sprinkle the stuffing mix over the top, and drizzle on the melted butter. Bake for 50 to 60 minutes, or until the chicken is done.

NOTE: I have found that if I use boneless chicken breasts I have to bake them for only about 45 to 50 minutes.

mama's old-fashioned stuffing

10 to 12 servings

*Boy, oh boy, does the smell of this stuffing bring back great
memories! It was the "special occasion" stuffing in our
house when I was a kid—in fact, it still is!*

⅔ cup vegetable oil

1 cup finely chopped celery
(about 4 stalks)

1¼ cups finely chopped onion
(about 2 small onions)

1½ cups finely chopped carrots
(about 3 carrots)

3 eggs, lightly beaten

1 package (14 ounces) cubed
herb-seasoned stuffing mix
(8 cups)

4 cups water

2 teaspoons salt

½ teaspoon pepper

Preheat the oven to 350°F. In a large skillet, heat the oil over
medium-high heat. Add the celery, onions, and carrots, and sauté
until light golden and limp, about 10 minutes. Let cool slightly.
Meanwhile, in a large bowl, combine the eggs, stuffing mix, water,
salt, and pepper, and mix until well blended and stuffing is soft.
Add the vegetable mixture to the stuffing mixture and mix well.
Place in a greased 9" × 13" baking pan and bake for about 1¼
hours, or until golden.

NOTE: I find it easier to use a food processor than to finely chop
the veggies by hand.

146

mashed potato stuffing

about 8 servings

Here's a variation on our traditional stuffing. Is it stuffing,
or is it potatoes? It's both! And it's a real treat
'cause it'll please everybody!

3 cups mashed potatoes	½ teaspoon pepper
1 teaspoon baking powder	2 tablespoons vegetable oil
4 cups herb-seasoned stuffing mix (1 14-ounce package contains 8 cups)	1 cup chopped onion
	½ cup sliced celery
¼ cup minced fresh parsley	½ teaspoon minced garlic
	1 cup chicken stock

Preheat the oven to 350°F. In a large bowl, combine the mashed potatoes and baking powder. Add the stuffing mix, parsley, and pepper; mix well. In a large skillet, heat the oil over medium heat; add the onion, celery, and garlic, and sauté for 10 to 15 minutes, or until the vegetables are tender. Add the vegetable mixture to the potato mixture; mix well, then add the chicken stock and mix well again. Place in a greased 2-quart casserole and bake for 30 to 35 minutes, or until the top is lightly browned. Remove from the oven and keep warm until ready to serve.

NOTE: Whether you use homemade or instant mashed potatoes, there's no need to add salt.

vegetable harvest stuffing

10 to 12 servings

With so many of my recipes, I give my mom well-deserved credit. This time, though, it goes to my wife. This is her standard stuffing recipe that our family and friends look forward to sharing with us at holiday gatherings. After you try it, you'll know why.

1 cup (2 sticks) butter or margarine	1½ cups chicken or turkey broth
2 cups sliced mushrooms	Salt to taste
1¼ cups chopped onion	Pepper to taste
1 cup chopped celery	1 package (14 ounces) cubed herb-seasoned stuffing mix (8 cups)
4 garlic cloves, chopped	
1 tablespoon dried basil	2½ cups shredded carrots
8 eggs, beaten	1 cup chopped fresh parsley

Preheat the oven to 350°F. In a large skillet, melt the butter over medium heat; sauté the mushrooms, onion, celery, garlic, and basil until the vegetables are limp, about 10 minutes. In a medium-sized bowl, combine the eggs, broth, salt, and pepper. Scatter the bread cubes in a large bowl or baking pan. Add the mushroom mixture and the egg mixture and toss gently to blend. Add the carrots and parsley and toss again. Scoop the stuffing into a greased 9" × 13" baking pan and bake for about 1 hour, or until golden and crisp.

NOTE: This should be enough to loosely stuff a 12- to 14-pound turkey (with a little left over) if you wish, but be sure to:

1. Refrigerate stuffing until ready to stuff and roast turkey.
2. Adjust cooking time and temperature accordingly.
3. Remove leftover stuffing from turkey immediately after dinner and refrigerate turkey and stuffing separately.

index

Almost-fried chicken, 61
Appetizers and first courses, 31–37
  chicken puffs, 32
  creamy tomato chicken spread, 36
  garlic chicken bites, 31
  garlic soup, 39
  Greek spinach soup, 38
  parsnip and spinach cream soup, 40
  party pizza, 35
  sesame chicken, 33–34
  turkey "everything," 100
  turkey stuffed mushrooms, 37
Apple salsa, chicken with, 132
Avocado melt, chicken, 128

Baked:
  almost-fried chicken, 61
  Cajun turkey, 98
  cheesy chicken, 88
  chicken divan, 75
  chicken in wine sauce, 76
  chicken "Normand-y," 78
  chicken puffs, 32
  cranberry chicken, 64
  crispy-coat chicken, 89
  crispy Parmesan chicken, 69
  Dijon chicken breasts, 83
  "don't peek" chicken, 73
  easy chicken, 141
  easy sweet 'n' sour chicken, 62
  Friday night roasted chicken, 138

garlic chicken bites, 31
garlic chicken Florentine, 86
garlicky chicken, 46
garlic roasted chicken, 71
herbed 'n' spiced chicken, 77
homestyle chicken, 143
honey chicken, 121
impossible chicken 'n' broccoli pie, 90
Italian chicken and rice, 110
Italian cutlets, 92
Louisiana chicken, 66
North African chicken, 129
nutty drummers, 126
oven-fried chicken, 142
party pizza, 35
peppered raspberry chicken, 134
poulet Marengo, 63
ranch chicken breasts, 133
roast chicken and kiwi with raspberry glaze, 122
simply good chicken, 82
taco turkey, 97
turkey meat loaf Florentine, 94
turkey mushroom meat loaf, 93
turkey Oscar, 91
turkey stuffed mushrooms, 37
Balsamic vinegar:
  chicken breasts with, 127
  marinated chicken, 47
Barbecue(d):
  chuck wagon mix, 118
  easy chicken, 141
  taco turkey, 97

Basil-tomato turkey sauce, 52
Bean(s):
　black-eyed pea skillet, 116
　chuck wagon mix, 118
　two-, turkey chili, 117
Beef:
　delicate and fancy marinade,
　　44
　easy chicken fricassee, 144
　turkey mushroom meat loaf,
　　93
Bistro chicken, 84
Bites, garlic chicken, 31
Black-eyed pea skillet, 116
Boneless products, buying of, 17
Boning, 21–22
Breasts, chicken, 20, 86, 111
　almost-fried, 61
　avocado melt, 128
　baked garlicky, 46
　balsamic marinated, 47
　with balsamic vinegar, 127
　bistro, 84
　boning of, 21–22
　cacciatore, new, 140
　cheesy baked, 88
　country goodness, 80
　delicate and fancy marinade
　　for, 44
　Dijon, 83
　divan, 75
　easy sweet 'n' sour, 62
　egg foo-yung, 124
　"fancee," 81
　fancy fast, 145
　Florentine, garlic, 86
　French, in wine sauce, 113
　garlic and hot pepper
　　marinade for, 43
　garlic bites, 31
　glazed, 87
　grilled chickabob, 49
　homestyle, 143
　Italian, 72
　Italian baked, 92
　lemon coat, 45
　with lemon sauce, 65

light lemon-dill, 85
marinades for, 43–44
Marsala, 139
"Normand-y," 78
poulet Marengo, 63
provolone, 130
ranch, 133
ratatouille, 105
roast, with curried honey
　mustard sauce, 131
roasting of, 23
and sausage, 107
sesame, 33–34
skillet, 111
spicy, 48
with summer vegetables, 109
sweet 'n' sour tenders, 70
tarragon, 106
teriyaki, 50
Thai, 123
in tomato Marsala sauce, 79
in wine sauce, 76
with zucchini and tomatoes,
　112
Breasts, turkey:
　Cajun, 98
　garlic and hot pepper
　　marinade for, 43
　marinade for, 43
　new potato salad with, 55
　strips, Super Bowl, 99
Broccoli:
　chicken divan, 75
　chicken in wine sauce, 76
　pie, impossible chicken 'n',
　　90
Broiled:
　baked garlicky chicken, 46
　chicken with apple salsa, 132
　glazed chicken breasts, 87
　lemon coat chicken, 45
　lighter burgers, 95
　light lemon-dill chicken, 85
　spicy chicken, 48
　teriyaki, chicken, 50
　turkey "pot roast," 96
Broilers, buying of, 17

Broth and stock, chicken:
  garlic soup, 39
  Greek spinach soup, 38
  mashed potato stuffing, 147
  parsnip and spinach cream
    soup, 40
  vegetable harvest stuffing, 148
Buffalo-style turkey wings, 102
Burgers, lighter, 95
Buying and preparing poultry,
    17, 18–19, 20

Cacciatore, new chicken, 140
Cajun:
  black-eyed pea skillet, 116
  crispy-coat chicken, 89
  turkey, 98
Cakes, turkey hash, 101
Cheese:
  baked chicken, 88
  crispy Parmesan chicken, 69
  impossible chicken 'n' broccoli
    pie, 90
  Italian chicken and rice, 110
  party pizza, 35
  provolone chicken, 130
Chili, two-bean turkey, 117
Chinese:
  chicken, 67
  chicken egg foo-yung, 124
  chicken fried rice, 125
Chuck wagon mix, 118
Company stew, 115
Cooked chicken:
  'n' broccoli pie, impossible, 90
  buying of, 17
  fried rice, 125
  puffs, 32
Country goodness chicken, 80
Cranberry chicken, 64
Creamy tomato chicken spread,
    36
Crispy-coat chicken, 89
Crispy Parmesan chicken, 69
Curried honey mustard sauce,
    roast chicken with, 131
Curry chicken, 108

Cutlets, chicken, 20
Cutlets, turkey:
  Italian baked, 92
  Mediterranean salad, 54
  Oscar, 91

Delicate and fancy marinade, 44
Dijon mustard:
  chicken breasts, 83
  lemon coat chicken, 45
Dill:
  lemon chicken, light, 85
  tomato turkey sauce, 52
Divan, chicken, 75
"Don't peek" chicken, 73
Drummettes, cutting of, 21–22
Drumsticks, chicken, 20
  nutty drummers, 126
  roasting of, 23
Drumsticks, turkey:
  "pot roast," 96
  taco, 97

Easy barbecued chicken, 141
Easy chicken fricassee, 144
Easy sweet 'n' sour chicken, 62
Egg foo-yung, chicken, 124

Family favorites, 135–48
  easy barbecued chicken, 141
  easy chicken fricassee, 144
  fancy fast chicken, 145
  Friday night roasted chicken,
    138
  homestyle chicken, 143
  Mama's chicken soup, 137
  Mama's old-fashioned stuffing,
    146
  Marsala chicken, 139
  mashed potato stuffing, 147
  new chicken cacciatore, 140
  oven-fried chicken, 142
  vegetable harvest stuffing, 149
Fancy fast chicken, 145
Florentine:
  garlic chicken, 86
  turkey meat loaf, 94

French:
  bistro chicken, 84
  chicken breasts in wine sauce, 113
  country chicken, 68
Friday night roasted chicken, 138
Fried:
  almost-, chicken, 61
  Buffalo-style wings, 102
  lighter burgers, 95
  oven-, chicken, 142
  rice, chicken, 125
  turkey hash cakes, 101
Fryers, buying of, 17

Garlic:
  baked chicken, 46
  chicken bites, 31
  chicken Florentine, 86
  hot pepper marinade, 43
  roasted chicken, 71
  soup, 39
Glaze(d):
  chicken breasts, 87
  raspberry, roast chicken and kiwi with, 122
Greek spinach soup, 38
Grilled:
  baked garlicky chicken, 46
  balsamic marinated chicken, 47
  chickabob, 49
  Dijon chicken breasts, 83
  easy barbecued chicken, 141
  lemon coat chicken, 45
  lighter burgers, 95
  taco turkey, 97
  teriyaki, chicken, 50
Ground chicken:
  buying of, 17
  spread, creamy tomato, 36
Ground turkey, 13
  black-eyed pea skillet, 116
  lighter burgers, 95
  meat loaf Florentine, 94

mushroom meat loaf, 93
spread, creamy tomato, 36

Hash cakes, turkey, 101
Herbed 'n' spiced chicken, 77
Homestyle chicken, 143
Honey:
  chicken, 121
  mustard sauce, roast chicken with curried, 131
Hot pepper and garlic marinade, 43

Impossible chicken 'n' broccoli pie, 90
Italian:
  baked cutlets, 92
  chicken, 72
  chicken and rice, 110
  chicken in tomato Marsala sauce, 79
  chicken with zucchini and tomatoes, 112
  crispy-coat chicken, 89
  garlic chicken Florentine, 86
  turkey meat loaf Florentine, 94
Italian sausage:
  chicken and, 107
  chicken livers and, 114
  party pizza, 35
  two-bean turkey chili, 117

Kiwi and roast chicken with raspberry glaze, 122

Leftover chicken, 19
  divan, 75
  impossible chicken 'n' broccoli pie, 90
  puffs, 32
Leftover turkey:
  Buffalo-style wings, 102
  divan, 75
  "everything," 100
  hash cakes, 101
  macaroni salad and, 53

Legs, chicken, 20
  with apple salsa, 132
  new chicken cacciatore, 140
  nutty drummers, 126
  peppered raspberry, 134
  roasting of, 23
Lemon:
  coat chicken, 45
  dill chicken, light, 85
  sauce, chicken with, 65
Lighter burgers, 95
Light lemon-dill chicken, 85
Livers, chicken, sausage and,
    114
Louisiana chicken, 66

Macaroni turkey salad, 53
Main courses, 57–134
  almost-fried chicken, 61
  bistro chicken, 58
  black-eyed pea skillet, 116
  Buffalo-style turkey wings,
    102
  Cajun turkey, 98
  cheesy baked chicken, 88
  chicken and sausage, 107
  chicken avocado melt, 128
  chicken breasts with balsamic
    vinegar, 127
  chicken divan, 75
  chicken easy, 74
  chicken egg foo-yung, 124
  chicken "fancee," 81
  chicken fried rice, 125
  chicken in tomato Marsala
    sauce, 79
  chicken in wine sauce, 76
  chicken Italian, 72
  chicken "Normand-y," 78
  chicken ratatouille, 105
  chicken with apple salsa, 132
  chicken with lemon sauce, 65
  chicken with summer
    vegetables, 109
  chicken with zucchini and
    tomatoes, 112
  Chinese chicken, 67

chuck wagon mix, 118
company stew, 115
country goodness chicken, 80
cranberry chicken, 64
crispy-coat chicken, 89
crispy Parmesan chicken, 69
curry chicken, 108
Dijon chicken breasts, 83
"don't peek" chicken, 73
easy barbecued chicken, 141
easy chicken fricassee, 144
easy sweet 'n' sour chicken,
    62
fancy fast chicken, 145
French chicken breasts in
    wine sauce, 113
French country chicken, 68
Friday night roasted chicken,
    138
garlic chicken Florentine, 86
garlic roasted chicken, 71
glazed chicken breasts, 87
herbed 'n' spiced chicken, 77
homestyle chicken, 143
honey chicken, 121
impossible chicken 'n' broccoli
    pie, 90
Italian baked cutlets, 92
Italian chicken and rice, 110
lighter burgers, 95
light lemon-dill chicken, 85
Louisiana chicken, 66
Marsala chicken, 139
new chicken cacciatore, 140
North African chicken, 129
nutty drummers, 126
"one pan," 105–18
oven-fried chicken, 142
peppered raspberry chicken,
    134
poulet Marengo, 63
provolone chicken, 130
ranch chicken breasts, 133
roast chicken and kiwi with
    rasberry glaze, 122
roast chicken with curried
    honey mustard sauce, 131

Main courses (*cont.*)
 sausage and chicken livers, 114
 simply good chicken, 82
 skillet chicken, 111
 Super Bowl turkey strips, 99
 sweet 'n' sour tenders, 70
 taco turkey, 97
 tarragon chicken breast, 106
 taste adventures, 60, 119–134
 Thai chicken, 123
 turkey "everything," 100
 turkey hash cakes, 101
 turkey meat loaf Florentine, 94
 turkey mushroom meat loaf, 93
 turkey Oscar, 91
 turkey "pot roast," 96
 two-bean turkey chili, 117
Mama's old-fashioned stuffing, 146
Marengo, poulet, 63
Marinades, marinated, 43–50
 baked garlicky chicken, 46
 balsamic chicken, 47
 chicken teriyaki, 50
 delicate and fancy, 44
 garlic and hot pepper, 43
 grilled chickabob, 49
 lemon coat chicken, 45
 poultry, 43
 sesame chicken, 33–34
 spicy chicken, 48
Marsala:
 chicken, 139
 tomato sauce, chicken in, 79
Mashed potato stuffing, 147
Measures, quick, 27
Meat loaf:
 Florentine, turkey, 94
 turkey mushroom, 93
Mediterranean turkey salad, 54
Mushroom(s):
 meat loaf, turkey and, 93
 turkey stuffed, 37
Mustard:
 Dijon chicken breasts, 83

honey sauce, curried, roast chicken with, 131
lemon coat chicken, 45

New chicken cacciatore, 140
New potato salad with turkey, 55
"Normand-y," chicken, 78
North African chicken, 129
Nutty drummers, 126

"One pans," 105–18
 black-eyed pea skillet, 116
 chicken and sausage, 107
 chicken ratatouille, 105
 chicken with summer vegetables, 109
 chicken with zucchini and tomatoes, 112
 chuck wagon mix, 118
 company stew, 115
 curry chicken, 108
 French chicken breasts in wine sauce, 113
 Italian chicken and rice, 110
 sausage and chicken livers, 114
 skillet chicken, 111
 tarragon chicken breast, 106
 two-bean turkey chili, 117
Oscar, turkey, 91
Oven-fried chicken, 142

Packaged foods, sizes of, 28
Parmesan chicken, crispy, 69
Parsnip and spinach cream soup, 40
Parts (pieces), chicken:
 buying of, 17
 Chinese, 67
 cranberry, 64
 crispy-coat, 89
 crispy Parmesan, 69
 curry, 108
 "don't peek," 73
 easy, 74
 easy barbecued, 141

French country, 68
garlic roasted, 71
herbed 'n' spiced, 77
homestyle, 143
honey, 121
Louisiana, 66
North African, 129
oven-fried, 142
and rice, Italian, 110
roasting of, 23
simply good, 82
soup, Mama's, 137
Party pizza, 35
Pea skillet, black-eyed, 116
Peppered raspberry chicken, 134
Pie, impossible chicken 'n' broccoli, 90
Pizza, party, 35
Potato salad, new, with turkey, 55
"Pot roast," turkey, 96
Poulet Marengo, 63
Poultry marinade, 43
Preparation tips, 18–19
Provolone chicken, 130
Puffs, chicken, 32

Quarters, roasting of, 23
Quick measures, 27

Ranch chicken breasts, 133
Raspberry:
  glaze, roast chicken and kiwi with, 122
  peppered chicken, 134
Ratatouille, chicken, 105
Rice:
  chuck wagon mix, 118
  Italian chicken and, 110
Roast chicken, 11
  with curried honey mustard sauce, 131
  Friday night, 138
  garlic, 71
  and kiwi with raspberry glaze, 122

timetable for, 23
Roaster, buying of, 17
Roasting a whole turkey, 24–26

Salads, 53–55
  Mediterranean turkey, 54
  new potato, with turkey, 55
  turkey macaroni, 53
Salsa, apple, chicken with, 132
Sandwich, sliced turkey, spread for, 51
Sauces:
  creamy tomato chicken spread, 36
  sliced turkey spread, 51
  tomato-basil turkey, 52
  see also Marinades, marinated
Sausage:
  chicken and, 107
  and chicken livers, 114
  chuck wagon mix, 118
  party pizza, 35
  turkey stuffed mushrooms, 37
  two-bean turkey chili, 117
Sautéed:
  black-eyed pea skillet, 116
  chicken and sausage, 107
  chicken breasts in wine sauce, 113
  chicken breasts with balsamic vinegar, 127
  chicken in tomato Marsala sauce, 79
  chicken Italian, 72
  chicken ratatouille, 105
  chicken with summer vegetables, 109
  chicken with zucchini and tomatoes, 112
  chuck wagon mix, 118
  company stew, 115
  creamy tomato chicken spread, 36
  curry chicken, 108
  French country chicken, 68
  Marsala chicken, 139

155

sautéed (*cont.*)
Mediterranean turkey salad, 54
sausage and chicken livers, 114
Super Bowl turkey strips, 99
sweet 'n' sour tenders, 70
tarragon chicken breast, 106
Thai chicken, 123
two-bean turkey chili, 117
Sesame chicken, 33–34
Shopping tips, 18
Side dishes:
fried rice, 125
Mama's old-fashioned stuffing, 146
mashed potato stuffing, 147
vegetable harvest stuffing, 148
Simply good chicken, 8
Skillet chicken, 111
Sliced turkey spread, 51
Soups, 38–40
garlic, 39
Greek spinach, 38
Mama's chicken, 137
parsnip and spinach cream, 40
Spicy chicken, 48
Spinach:
garlic chicken Florentine, 86
Greek soup, 38
and parsnip cream soup, 40
turkey meat loaf Florentine, 94
Spreads:
creamy tomato chicken, 36
sliced turkey, 51
turkey "everything," 100
Stew, company, 115
Stock, *see* Broth and stock, chicken
Stuffed mushrooms, turkey, 37
Stuffing, 19
crispy-coat chicken, 89
herbed 'n' spiced chicken, 77
Mama's old-fashioned, 146
mashed potato, 147
vegetable harvest stuffing, 148

Substitutions, 27–28
Super Bowl turkey strips, 99
Sweet 'n' sour:
chicken, easy, 62
tenders, 70

Taco turkey, 97
Tarragon chicken breast, 106
Taste adventures, 119–34
chicken avocado melt, 128
chicken breasts with balsamic vinegar, 127
chicken egg foo-yung, 124
chicken fried rice, 125
chicken with apple salsa, 132
honey chicken, 121
North African chicken, 19
nutty drummers, 16
peppered raspberry chicken, 134
provolone chicken, 130
ranch chicken breasts, 133
roast chicken and kiwi with raspberry glaze, 122
roast chicken with curried honey mustard sauce, 131
Thai chicken, 123
Tenderloins, chicken, 70
Teriyaki, chicken, 50
Thai chicken, 123
Thighs, chicken, 20
with apple salsa, 132
cacciatore, new, 140
roasting of, 23
Tomato(es):
basil turkey sauce, 52
chicken spread, creamy, 36
chicken with zucchini and, 112
Marsala sauce, chicken in, 79
Turkey, 11
company stew, 115
"everything," 100
hash cakes, 101
macaroni salad, 53
roasting of, 24–26
sliced, spread for, 51

tomato-basil sauce for, 52
vegetable harvest stuffing for,
    148
wings, Buffalo-style, 102
Turkey, ground, 13
    black-eyed pea skillet, 116
    lighter burgers, 95
    meat loaf Florentine, 94
    mushroom meat loaf, 93
    spread, creamy tomato, 36
Turkey, leftover:
    Buffalo-style wings, 102
    divan, 75
    "everything," 100
    hash cakes, 101
    macaroni salad and, 53
Turkey breasts:
    Cajun, 98
    garlic and hot pepper
        marinade for, 43
    marinade for, 43
    new potato salad with, 55
    strips, Super Bowl, 99
Turkey cutlets:
    Italian baked, 92
    Mediterranean salad, 54
    Oscar, 91
Turkey drumsticks:
    "pot roast," 96
    taco, 97

Turkey sausage:
    chuck wagon mix, 118
    party pizza, 35
    stuffed mushrooms, 37
    two-bean chili, 117
Two-bean turkey chili, 117

Vegetable(s):
    harvest stuffing, 148
    summer, chicken with, 109

Whole chicken:
    buying of, 17, 20
    Friday night roasted, 138
    roasting of, 23
Wine:
    chicken in tomato Marsala
        sauce, 79
    Marsala chicken, 139
    sauce, chicken in, 76
    sauce, French chicken breasts
        in, 113
Wing(s), chicken, 20
    drummettes, cutting of, 21–22
    fricassee, easy, 144
Wings, Buffalo-style turkey, 102

Zucchini and tomatoes, chicken
    with, 112

ABOUT THE AUTHOR

Art Ginsburg is best known as TV's lovable cooking celebrity, MR. FOOD®. His popular food news insert segment is the largest in the nation, seen in over 260 cities.

Twelve years ago Art became MR. FOOD®, but long before that his life centered around food — and family. From running the family butcher shop to establishing the family catering business, Art has cultivated his many successes with his family by his side. Art's wife and three children all continue to work with him now in producing the MR. FOOD® television show, and his granddaughters appear to be Pop-Pop's three most enthusiastic fans.

Get All Five Books
in the Mr. Food® Library!

WILLIAM MORROW

ENJOY THE *ENTIRE*
MR. FOOD®
EXPERIENCE!

Why be satisfied with just a "taste" when you can have the entire "meal"? Once you've experienced any one of **MR. FOOD®'s** easy, tantalizing recipes, you'll want to try all of them! All you have to do is use this handy form to order lots more **OOH it's so GOOD!!**™ (*And if you purchase 3 or more books with this order, you get a bonus discount of $1.00 off the price of each book!*)

Please indicate the quantity of each **MR. FOOD®** Cookbook that you wish to order:

_____ The **MR. FOOD®** Cookbook, OOH it's so GOOD!!™ @ $12.95 each: $ _____

_____ **MR. FOOD®** Cooks Like Mama @ $12.95 each: _____

_____ **MR. FOOD®** Cooks Chicken @ $9.95 each: _____

_____ **MR. FOOD®** Cooks Pasta @ $9.95 each: _____

_____ **MR. FOOD®** Makes Dessert @ $9.95 each: _____

+$2.00 <u>PER BOOK</u> Shipping & Handling
(*Canadian Orders add additional
$2.00 per book*)   _____

SUBTOTAL   _____

*Less $1.00 per book if
ordering 3 or more books*   _____

+ Applicable Sales Tax
(*FL Residents Only*)   _____

TOTAL - *In U.S. Funds* $ _____

Make check out to **MR. FOOD®** and send to: **MR. FOOD®**, P.O. Box 16216, Plantation, FL, 33318-6216

Method of Payment: _____ Check or Money Order Enclosed

_____ Credit Card: _____ Visa _____ Mastercard

Expiration Date _____

Signature _____

Account # | | | | | | | | | | | | | | | | | | |

PLEASE ALLOW 6 TO 8 WEEKS FOR DELIVERY.